COMPUTER STUDIES SERIES

General Editor:
Donald Leach, B.Sc., F.I.M.A., M.B.C.S., M.Inst.P.
Napier College of Science and Technology Edinburgh

FORTRAN
FOR BEGINNERS

by Roy Court
Stationers' Company's School London

illustrated by Edward Burrill

Holmes McDougall Edinburgh

First Published 1970

Published by Holmes McDougall Ltd.,
137 Leith Walk,
Edinburgh EH6 8NS.

Set in "Monophoto" Univers.
Printed in Great Britain by Banks & Co.

Standard Book Number 7157 0824-4

7157 0824—4

PREFACE

With the rapid increase in the number of computers, and their increasing impact in many aspects of everyday life, many secondary schools have recently introduced computer studies into their curriculum.

One of the difficulties encountered is that most computing books have tended to be aimed at undergraduate level and above, and there is a lack of suitable books for school use. This book, which is based on extensive class-room experience, has been written for the 14–16 year old, but could be used by 6th formers, students in Further Education, Polytechnics, Universities, and indeed anyone wishing to acquire a knowledge of FORTRAN. Several sections of the book, and some of the problems, deal with certain of the more advanced aspects of FORTRAN which may be studied in the 6th form. To gain full benefit from this course, however, no previous knowledge of computing is required,* and only a basic knowledge of elementary arithmetic and algebra is needed for most of the work in the book. (The more difficult paragraphs and assignments are indicated by an asterisk.)

The material in the book is arranged so that pupils with access to computing facilities can start writing programs almost immediately. The input and output of numbers is dealt with first, followed by arithmetic calculations. Each new aspect of FORTRAN is illustrated with programs which have been processed on a computer, both the input and output being shown. As far as possible, the programs have been simplified so as to illustrate clearly the point under discussion.

Since most computers are used for commercial rather than scientific work, many of the programs in the book are of a simple "data processing" type; that is, they can perform relatively simple operations on large quantities of data. They have not been made too realistic where this would tend to obscure the main points of the program.

To simplify the treatment, certain features of FORTRAN have been omitted. For example, the arithmetic IF statement has been excluded, but it can usually be replaced by logical IF statements.

* For a readable introduction to computer studies see *Primer of Computing* by Donald Leach and Bob Bowker, a companion volume in this series.

CONTENTS

		Page
	PREFACE	3
UNIT 1	INTRODUCTION	7
1.2	How a Computer is used	7
1.3	How to use this book	9
1.4	The various versions of FORTRAN	10
UNIT 2	PROGRAMMING A COMPUTER TO READ AND WRITE NUMBERS	
2.1	Real numbers	11
2.2	A FORTRAN Program	12
2.3	The READ Statement	13
2.4	The FORMAT Statement	14
2.5	The WRITE Statement	16
2.6	The END Statement and *DATA	17
2.7	Rounding up Answers	17
2.8	Reserved Words	18
2.9	Comment Lines	18
2.10	Punching a Program correctly	18
UNIT 3	ARITHMETIC WITH FORTRAN	
3.1	Multiplication, Division, Addition and Subtraction	19
3.2	Powers of Numbers (Exponentiation)	20
3.3	Use of Brackets in FORTRAN	21
3.4	Mistakes in Arithmetic Assignment Statements	22
3.5	The Square Root Function	22
3.6	Finding Errors in Programs	24
3.7	*The Order in which Operations are performed	25
UNIT 4	MORE ABOUT CALCULATIONS IN FORTRAN	
4.1	Use of Names for Variables	27
4.2	How to shorten FORMAT Statements	28
UNIT 5	INTEGER NUMBERS	29
5.2	The FORMAT Statements needed with INTEGERS	29
5.3	INTEGER Names	30
5.4	INTEGERS in Arithmetic Assignment Statements	31
5.5	Mixing REAL and INTEGER Numbers	32
5.6	Changing the value of a variable in a Program	34

UNIT 6 MAKING DECISIONS IN PROGRAMS
6.1 CONDITIONAL Statements 35
6.2 The GREATER THAN Statement 35
6.3 Other Conditional Statements 35
6.4 Loops, GO TO and STOP Statements 37
6.5 The use of a Loop in a Data Processing Problem 38

UNIT 7 THE USE OF DO LOOPS 41
7.2 An Example of the DO Statement in Data Processing 43
7.3 Producing REAL Numbers with a DO Statement 44
7.4 Producing Decimal Numbers with DO Statements 45
7.5 The Average of a series of numbers using a DO Statement 46
7.6 Another Example of a DO Statement used in Data Processing 47
7.7 An Example of a Conditional Statement in a DO Loop 49
7.8 DO LOOPS of variable size 50

UNIT 8 MORE ADVANCED USE OF FORMAT STATEMENTS—CONTINUATION LINES AND OVERFLOW
8.1 Input and Output of more than one line with a single FORMAT Statement 52
8.2 The use of / in Input and Output 55
8.3 Continuation Lines 56
8.4 Overflow 57

UNIT 9 ARRAYS
9.1 Input and Output of Arrays 58
9.2 The use of DO Statements with Arrays 59
9.3 The SUM of the Members of an Array 61

UNIT 10 PRODUCING TITLES AND HEADINGS
10.1 Hollerith Output 63
10.2 Producing Blanks in Output 66

UNIT 11 PRINTING HEADINGS AND NUMBERS TOGETHER
11.1 The FORMAT Statement required 68
11.2 *An Example of Hollerith Output in Commercial Programming 70
11.3 *Spacing to the start of a new page 71

UNIT 12 MORE ABOUT FORTRAN FUNCTIONS 73
12.2 The SIN Function 73
12.3 Making Numbers Positive 74
12.4 *Finding a Square Root by Successive Approximation 74

UNIT 13 MORE ABOUT DO LOOPS
13.1 The use of two DO Statements 76
13.2 Nested DO Loops 77
13.3 Providing Headings 79
13.4 Multiple DO Loops 81

UNIT 14 MORE ABOUT ARRAYS
14.1 Two-dimensional Arrays 82
14.2 To Print a row or a column from an Array 83
14.3 The Sum of a row or a column from an Array 85
14.4 *The use of an Array in a Data Processing problem 86
14.5 *To Read a large Array 87
14.6 Type Statements 88

*UNIT 15 HANDLING CHARACTERS AND DRAWING GRAPHS
15.1 Introduction 89
15.2 A Data Processing Example 90
15.3 Drawing Graphs using a Computer 92
15.4 Plotting Graphs with fractional and negative values for Y 95

UNIT 16 THE USE OF STATEMENT FUNCTIONS IN PROGRAMS
16.1 98
16.2 Statement Functions of more than one variable 99
16.3 *Solution of a pair of Simultaneous Equations using Statement Functions 100
16.4 Rules for using Statement Functions 100

*UNIT 17 FUNCTION SUBPROGRAMS AND SUB-ROUTINE SUBPROGRAMS
17.1 Function Subprograms 102
17.2 A Function Subprogram using an Array 104
17.3 Subroutine Subprograms 105

SOLUTIONS 108

PROGRAMMER: R.COURT

DATE: 10.3.69 PAGE 1 OF 1

TITLE: SPECIMEN PROGRAM

STATEMENT NO.	

```
      READ(2,1)X,Y,Z
    1 FORMAT(3F10.4)
      U=SQRT(3.0*X+2.0*Y+4.0*Z)
      WRITE(3,2)U
    2 FORMAT(1H ,F10.4)
      END
*DATA
   17.67          9.4       143.209
```

Introduction

UNIT
1

1.1 Computers are becoming vitally necessary in many situations in business and science: for example, the calculation of weekly wages in large business concerns, weather forecasting, controlling the operation of oil refineries, the design of aeroplanes, the National Giro and Income Tax collection. The number of computers in use is expected to grow rapidly over the next few years, and there are few people now living who can expect to go through the rest of their lives without being affected by the computer revolution. A computer is a highly complex electronic device which has been designed to carry out high speed calculations and to store a large quantity of information. It is able to do this, however, only if it receives the proper instructions. The instructions which are given to a computer are called the **program.**

Programs are written in a computer programming language, of which there are several, such as FORTRAN, ALGOL and COBOL. FORTRAN and ALGOL are used mainly for scientific work, while commercial programs are often written in COBOL. This book is aimed at teaching FORTRAN, and no previous knowledge of computer programming is necessary. Most of the mathematics that you will need in reading this book is very simple. The book does not teach everything there is to know about FORTRAN, but the main uses of the language are covered. If you read this book carefully and work through most of the assignments, you should be able to go on to more advanced books on FORTRAN.

1.2 How a Computer is used

Before you learn to write a program in FORTRAN, let us consider what happens when a computer is used to solve a problem. In many cases the person writing the program (i.e. the **programmer**) first draws a **flowchart** which breaks the problem down into a series of simple steps. You will see examples of flow charts when you start learning how to write programs in Unit 3. The program is written on a coding form and is shown opposite.

The program must then be prepared for **reading** by the computer and is reproduced on a machine which looks rather like a large typewriter and which punches cards, one for each line in the program. The computer takes its instruction from the pattern of holes punched in the card, but often as a check each card also has printed along the top the line which has been punched on it. Here is what the punched card containing the third line from our coding form would look like:

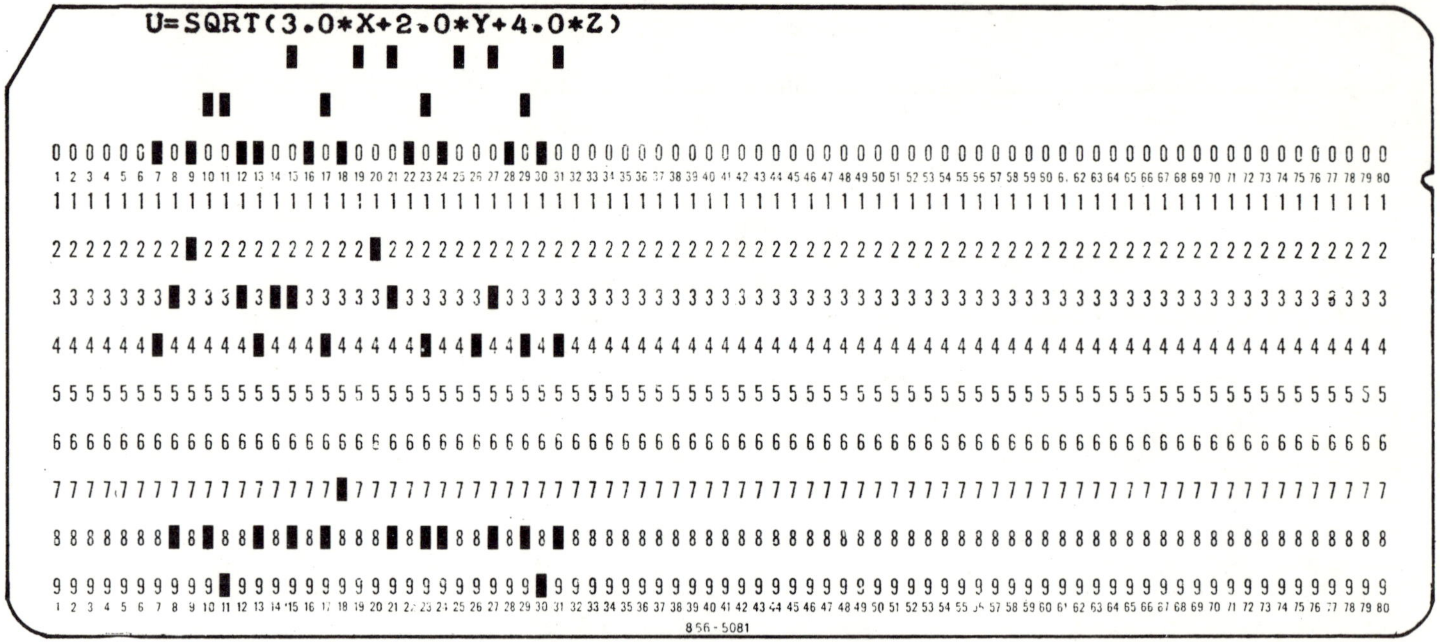

Some computers read programs which are punched on paper tape; a suitable machine for punching this tape is the **teleprinter,** which also produces a printed copy of the program. The printed copy, like the printing on the punched cards, can be used to check that the program has been punched correctly. Here is a part of the tape containing the program on the coding form, together with the typed copy of the line that it contains:

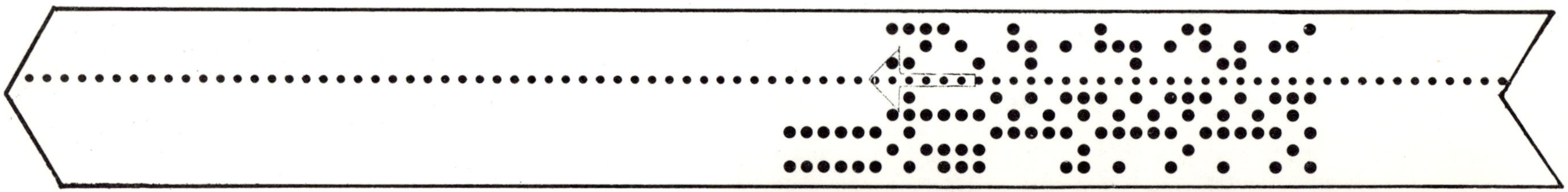

U=SQRT(3.0*X+2.0*Y+4.0*Z)

The cards or tape are then placed in the **reader** of the computer, which uses electrical equipment to **read** the program from the holes in the cards or tape. The computer will then **compile** the program. This means that the computer will translate the program from FORTRAN into a program in **machine language.** The program in machine language contains the same instructions, but it is now in a form which the computer can use. This is rather similar to a person being given written instructions in a language he cannot read. These instructions would have to be translated into English, so that he could follow them. Machine codes are difficult for humans to use, so special languages like FORTRAN have been devised to simplify the programmer's task.

When the computer compiles the program, it also looks for errors and prints out error messages. (This is dealt with in more detail at the end of Unit 3.) If the program is free from errors, the computer can carry out the instructions in the program; we call this **executing** the program. Finally the computer will print the results which the program was designed to produce.

The results may be printed by either of the two common forms of **output device,** a high-speed paper tape punch or a line printer. The paper tape produced by the punch has to be converted to a printed form by passing the tape through the reader of a teleprinter. Unlike the high-speed punch, the line-printer prints the output directly (i.e. the output is ready to read, without needing any further processing). Most line printers are much faster than paper tape punches, and can accommodate a longer line of type.
Whenever you read *line printer* in this book, you can assume that a paper tape output fed through a teleprinter will produce the same results.

When they output the results, most computers also produce a **listing** of the program. This listing is a printed copy of the program, and is most useful for checking against the original program on the coding form.

Most of the programs in this book have been run on a computer using paper tape input, and for each program photographic reproductions of both the program and the results are provided. A standard layout is used, with flow chart provided where necessary, and output appearing beneath the program.

1.3 How to use this book

Each unit deals with one or two parts of FORTRAN, and the units are further divided into sections. There are frequent sets of assignments, and you should do some of each set before you read the next section. Some parts of the book are rather harder than the rest, and these are marked like this *.

There are a large number of complete programs reproduced in this book. If you are writing a program of your own and you are having some difficulty, it may help if you look to see how a similar problem has been solved. For example, if you wished to produce your results in the form of a graph, and you had forgotten exactly how a computer has to be programmed to do this, you could look at Unit 15, where there are two such programs.

You will see that many of the programs in the book solve elementary problems that could be done much more quickly without a computer. The reason for this is simply that the book is designed to show you how to use the different parts of FORTRAN, not how to do difficult calculations. After you have worked through this book, you will be able to use FORTRAN in solving many complex problems with the aid of a computer.

1.4 The various versions of FORTRAN

There are many different makes of computer using FORTRAN, and each of them uses a slightly different kind of FORTRAN. The programs written in this book are in the version of ASA† FORTRAN IV which is used with the Honeywell 200 computers. You will find that if you use a computer which accepts a different version of FORTRAN, you can learn the main differences in a few minutes.

† American Standards Association.

Programming a Computer to Read and Write Numbers

UNIT
2

In this Unit you will learn how to prepare simple FORTRAN programs that will read in and print out numbers. In the next Unit you will be shown how to program a computer to carry out calculations.

2.1 Real Numbers

In computing, the term **real number** is used for any number with a decimal point. At this stage in writing a FORTRAN program all the numbers that you use must be real numbers, even if they are whole numbers. For example, when the numbers 0.46; 6.5; 23.0; 23,456; 7 682; are used in a program, you will have to write them as follows: 0.46; 6.5; 23.0; 23456.0; 7682.0. You will see that the first three of these numbers are unchanged, but the last two are written with decimal points. You should also notice that the comma has been removed from 23,456 and the space (the modern equivalent of the comma) from the last number. In FORTRAN, numbers are never written with a comma or a space. The semi-colons would, of course, not appear on the coding form.

It is possible to use numbers without points in FORTRAN programs; these are called **integer** numbers. Integer numbers will be studied in Unit 5.

ASSIGNMENT 2.1

Write the following numbers as you would write them as real numbers in a FORTRAN program.

1. 45.6	**4. 34.67**	**7. 2 867 109**
2. 57	**5. 1,400**	**8. 1**
3. 12,345	**6. 45,678.57**	**9. 243.5**

2.2 A FORTRAN Program

Most FORTRAN programs consist of three parts:

(1) instructions to the computer to read in or input certain numbers;

(2) instructions to the computer to carry out calculations with these numbers;

(3) instructions to the computer to write out or print out the answer.

If you look at Program 2.1, you will see a very simple program which reads in three numbers and prints them in reverse order. When you have read up to section 2.5 in this Unit, you should look at this program again, and you will then be able to see exactly how it works.

Here is how the program would look written by hand on a coding form.

PROGRAMMER R.COURT

TITLE **Specimen Read and Write Program**

DATE PAGE 1 OF 1

```
C     PROGRAM 2.1
      READ(2,1)P,Q,R
    1 FORMAT(F5.2,F5.2,F5.2)
      WRITE(3,6)R,Q,P
    6 FORMAT(1H ,F5.2,F5.2,F5.2)
      END
*DATA
+3.67-2.64+7.93
```

In a FORTRAN program, spacing is very important. You will see, for example, that most of the lines in the program start in column 7, and to ensure that the spacing is correct, you should use coding forms when you write your programs.

Here is the listing of the program, and underneath is the output. The listing, as explained in Unit 1, is produced by the computer after the program has been compiled.

```
C     PROGRAM 2.1
      READ(2,1)P,Q,R
    1 FORMAT(F5.2,F5.2,F5.2)
      WRITE(3,6)R,Q,P
    6 FORMAT(1H ,F5.2,F5.2,F5.2)
      END
*DATA
+3.67-2.64+7.93
```

```
 7.93-2.64 3.67
```

Let us now examine the main features of this program.

2.3 The READ Statement

The first part of a program instructs the computer to read in or input the numbers that it will need in the calculation. A **READ** statement is written like this.

```
      READ(2,1)P,Q,R
*DATA
+3.67-2.64+7.93
```

When the computer is presented with this **READ** statement, it takes it as an instruction to read in the three numbers after ***DATA,** giving **P** the value + 3.67, **Q** the value − 2.64, and **R** the value + 7.93. Note that the numbers in the data must follow the same order as the letters **P, Q, R,** and that the items of data must always be preceded by ***DATA** (or a similar statement, depending on the computer system being used).

In writing a FORTRAN program you can use any letters to stand for any numbers, except that for the moment **I, J, K, L, M, N** must not be used. You will learn about these letters when you deal with integers in Unit 5.

You will see that **READ** is followed by (2,1); the purpose of this is explained in section 2.4.

Here is another example of a **READ** statement.

```
      READ(2,1)A,X,Y,Z
*DATA
 5.0 5.78-5.67 6.0
```

In this case the computer will give **A** the value 5.0, **X** the value 5.78 and so on. You will see that this time the + signs have been left out. This is allowable, and in fact people writing programs will not normally put them in. But you must remember to leave a blank space where the + sign should be. The minus sign, however, must always be included.

It is a rule of FORTRAN that all statements, for example **READ,** must start in column 7, and that ***DATA** must start in column 1.

Look at the punctuation in the last two examples. All the letters after **READ** have a comma between them, but there is nothing after the last letter. If you put a comma or a full stop after the last letter, the computer will reject your program and print out an error message.

2.4 The FORMAT Statement

A **READ** statement is always followed by brackets containing two numbers, in our example (2,1). The first number tells the computer whether the data (the number to be used in the calculation) will be read from paper tape, from punched cards, or from the keyboard of the computer. In this book the first number will always be 2, the number of the tape reader unit, because all the data has been punched on paper tape. When you run programs on a computer, you will be given the necessary information about the number to use in the **FORMAT** statement.

The second number tells the computer to look for the **FORMAT** statement with that number in front of it. A number in front of a statement is called a **statement number.**

Here is the **FORMAT** statement of our program, together with the **READ** statement.

```
      READ(2,1)P,Q,R
    1 FORMAT(F5.2,F5.2,F5.2)
*DATA
 3.67-2.64 7.93
```

The purpose of a **FORMAT** statement is to tell the computer how the numbers it has to read are positioned, and how many places there are after the decimal point in each number.

The first **F5.2** states that the first number is in the first five spaces on the line, and that there are two figures after the point. The second **F5.2** states that the second number is in the next five spaces on the line, and that there are two figures after the point. Similarly for the third number. Again you will see in the ***DATA** that spaces have to be left for the + signs in front of the first and third numbers.

Here is another example of a **FORMAT** statement.
You will see that this time we have given the **FORMAT** statement the statement number 7. You may use any whole number as a statement number in front of the **FORMAT** statement provided the same number is used in the appropriate **READ** statement.

```
      READ(2,7)S,T
    7 FORMAT(F10.5,F6.3)
*DATA
  23.46   -3.46
```

The **F10.5** in this **FORMAT** statement tells the computer that the first number will be found in the first ten spaces, with spaces for five figures to the right of the point. The **F6.3** tells the computer that the second number will be found in the next six spaces, with spaces for three figures after the point.

You will see that neither of the numbers we have used fills up all the spaces provided for them. The first number uses only two of the five spaces allocated for figures after the point. This means that there will be three blank spaces at the end of the number. The second number uses only two of the three spaces allocated for figures after the point; this will leave one blank space at the end of the number.

Many FORTRAN programs are used several times, often with numbers of different length. You should therefore allow enough space in your **FORMAT** statements for the largest and smallest numbers that your program will have to deal with. If, for example, your program had to deal with numbers no larger than 5 000, with two figures after the point, you could say that the largest number that your program had to deal with was 5 000 and the smallest 0.01. On your coding form you would need one space for the sign, four spaces for the figures in front of the point, one space for the point, and two spaces for the figures after the point. This gives a total of eight spaces, and so you would need to use **F8.2** in your **FORMAT** statement. (You might, of course, use **F10.3,** but you must not use less than **F8.2.**)

ASSIGNMENT 2.2

1. Give the **FORMAT** statement, using the least number of spaces, which would allow the numbers in the range 0.001 to 10 000 to be read.

2. Give the **FORMAT** statement, using the least number of spaces, which would allow the numbers in the range 0.000 07 to 500 to be read.

3. Give the **FORMAT** statement, using the least number of spaces, which would allow the numbers in the range − 2 000.000 to 8 000.000 to be read.

4. Make a copy of the following program segment on a blank coding form. Complete it by inserting − 45.67 and 357.567 as values for **X** and **Y**.

```
      READ(2,10)X,Y
   10 FORMAT(F10.3,F10.3)
*DATA
```

5. Make a copy of the following program segment on a blank coding form. Complete it by inserting 0.56; 0.78; − 0.009 as values for **P, Q** and **R**.

```
      READ(2,5)P,Q,R
    5 FORMAT(F5.2,F5.2,F10.4)
*DATA
```

6. Find the errors in the following program segment and write a correct version.

```
      READ(2,8)A,B,C,
    8 FORMAT(F10.4,F12.4 F12.4,)
*DATA
   -24     +1,643.2       +36.4546
```

7. Find the errors in the following program segment and write a correct version.

```
      READ(2,7)P Q R
    8 FORMAT(F10.4,F10.4)
*DATA
    3.1       3.2       3.3
```

2.5 The WRITE Statement

```
      WRITE(3,6)R,Q,P
    6 FORMAT(1H ,F5.2,F5.2,F5.2)
```

All the programs in this book contain a **WRITE** statement which tells the computer to print out or output the results. Here is the **WRITE** statement from program 2.1.

When the computer comes to this **WRITE** statement, it takes it as an instruction to print out or output the values of **R, Q** and **P,** in our example + 7.93, − 2.64 and + 3.67.

Every **WRITE** statement contains two numbers in brackets which serve a similar purpose to that of the two numbers in the **READ** statement. The first number will vary with the computer that you are using. In this book it will always be 3, as this is the code number of the line printer used for all the outputs shown here.

The second number tells the computer to look for the **FORMAT** statement with that number in front of it. The **FORMAT** statement will tell the computer exactly how it has to space the numbers that you tell it to print. The **FORMAT** statement that we are considering has four parts; each has its specific purpose:

1H tells the computer that it has to print the values of **R, Q** and **P** at the start of a new line. Notice that in our programs **1H** must always be followed by a blank space to ensure that the numbers are printed on a new line.

F5.2 tells the computer that it has to print the first number in the first five spaces or print positions, with two places after the decimal point.

F5.2 tells the computer to print the second number in the second five spaces or print positions, with two places after the decimal point.

F5.2 tells the computer to print the third number in the third five spaces or print positions, with two places after the decimal point.
The output is spaced like this
b7.93|—2.64|b3.67
(Here b represents a blank space and would not, of course, be printed; neither would the vertical lines used to separate the numbers.)

Here is another example of a **WRITE** statement:

```
      WRITE(3,7)A,B
    7 FORMAT(1H ,F5.2,F10.4)
```

If **A** and **B** had the values 4.3 and 456.73 respectively, then the output would be spaced as follows:
b4.30|bb456.7300

ASSIGNMENT 2.3

If **A; B; C; D** have the values 45.78; − 0.78; 456.1; − 5.99, write down the output that these **WRITE** statements will produce. Use b to indicate blanks.

```
1.      WRITE (3,8)A,B
      8 FORMAT(1H ,F6.2,F6.2)
2.      WRITE(3,1)D,A
      1 FORMAT(1H ,F10.4,F8.4)
3.      WRITE(3,7)B,C,D
      7 FORMAT(1H ,F7.4,F8.3,F10.5)
```

If you now look back at Program 2.1, which reads three numbers and then prints them in reverse order, you will be able to see how it works.

2.6 The END Statement and *DATA

It is a FORTRAN rule that the last instruction in a program must be **END**.* This tells the computer that you have no more instructions to give it and that it can start on the calculation. The only entry after **END** is ***DATA** and the numbers that you wish to read. Later in the book, programs will be considered which do not have any data to be read, but some computers still need ***DATA** to be included, and so we will continue to insert ***DATA** in all the programs in this book.

2.7 Rounding up Answers

If the number that the computer outputs has more figures after the decimal point than you have allowed for in your **FORMAT** statement, the number

*Some computers also require the use of a **STOP** instruction – this is the last instruction to be executed but is not necessarily placed immediately before the **END** instruction.

will be rounded up when it is printed. For example, **F7.3** will print 25.248 as 25.248, but **F7.2** will print it as 25.25. In the same way **F7.4** will print 3.45458 as 3.4546, and **F7.2** will print 47.5349 as 47.53.*

2.8 Reserved Words

You will see that certain words in this book, such as **READ, WRITE, FORMAT** and **END,** are always printed in capital letters when they refer to parts of a program. These words have special uses in FORTRAN and are called **reserved words.** You will be meeting others as you read the book.

ASSIGNMENT 2.4

1. Write a program to input the numbers 1.2; 2.3; 3.4 and 4.5 and to output them in reverse order. Use **F5.1** in your **FORMAT** statements.
2. Write a program to input the numbers 2.57 and 3.75 and to output them rounded up to the first decimal place.
3. Find the mistakes in the following program and write a correct version.

```
      READ(3,4)X,M
    4 FORMAT(F5.2,F5.2)
      WRITE(2,5)M,X
    5 FORMAT(F5.2,F5.2)
      END
*DATA
 5.57-5.67
```

2.9 Comment Lines

As computers usually process dozens of programs at a time, it is necessary for the output to have a name or a title on each set of results, so that they can be returned to the person who sent in the program. One way of doing this is by means of the comment line. If, when a program is punched, the letter C is punched in column one, you may then write your name or title on the rest of the line. The computer will ignore this line when it is running the program, but will print it out on the listing. You may use a comment line at any point in a program. You will see that most of the programs in this book have comment lines, often for headings.

2.10 Punching a Program correctly

When you are punching a program, it is most important not to confuse the letter **O** with the number **0**, or to confuse the letter **I** with the number **1.** If you make this mistake, the computer will reject your program. With some computing equipment you may find that the letter **O** is printed as **Ø,** and with others the number zero is printed as **Ø.**

*For a format **Fn.m, n** will have a maximum value which is fixed by the computer system, for example 13, giving 11 significant figures plus sign and decimal point. Those requiring greater accuracy should examine **double precision** numbers.

Arithmetic with FORTRAN

UNIT
3

3.1 Multiplication, Division, Addition and Subtraction

You have learned in the last Unit how to instruct a computer to read in and print out numbers; in this Unit you will be shown how to instruct a computer to carry out arithmetical calculations.

If you look at Program 3.1, you will see a program to read in two real numbers, add them, and print out the two numbers followed by their sum. The output is shown underneath the program.

```
C     PROGRAM 3.1
      READ(2,10)X,Y
   10 FORMAT(F10.4,F10.4)
      Z=X+Y
      WRITE(3,11)X,Y,Z
   11 FORMAT(1H ,F10.4,F10.4,F10.4)
      END
*DATA
      7.3           2.7
```

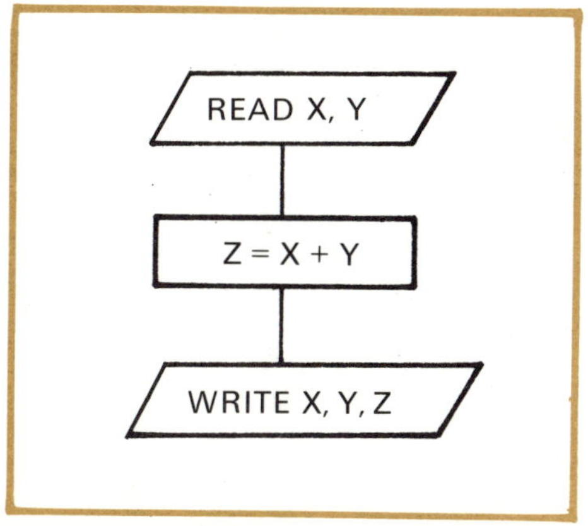


```
C       PROGRAM 3.1
        READ(2,10)X,Y
     10 FORMAT(F10.4,F10.4)
        Z=X+Y
        WRITE(3,11)X,Y,Z
     11 FORMAT(1H ,F10.4,F10.4,F10.4)
        END
*DATA
      7.3         2.7
```

```
    7.3000      2.7000     10.0000
```

This program has to do three main things:

1. **READ** the two numbers;
2. **add** the two numbers;
3. **WRITE** the output.

The flow chart for this program is shown (although for such a simple program you would not usually produce a flow chart).

Notice the shape of the boxes used for the **READ, WRITE,** and arithmetic statements in the flow chart. These are standard symbols.

The line **Z** = **X** + **Y** is an example of an **arithmetic assignment statement.** The computer will take from its **memory** the values of **X** and **Y,** add them together and give, or assign, the sum to **Z.** In this case the value of **Z** will be 10.0.

If, instead of adding the two numbers in the program, we wish to subtract, multiply, or divide them, the arithmetic assignment statements will look like this:

Z = X − Y
Z = X*Y
Z = X/Y

In FORTRAN you must always use * instead of the multiplication sign and / instead of ÷. You cannot write XY to mean X times Y as you do in algebra; you must write **X * Y.**

Here are some examples of arithmetic assignment statements. In all of them **A, B, C** are given the values 10.0, 5.0, 3.0 respectively.

G = A + 6.0	This would give **G** the value 16.0
P = A + B − C	This would give **P** the value 12.0
R = A*B*C	This would give **R** the value 150.0
T = A/B	This would give **T** the value 2.0
W = 7.0*A	This would give **W** the value 70.0
S = 2.0*A − C	This would give **S** the value 17.0

It is also permissible to write statements like **Y** = **4.0** + **6.0.** This would give **Y** the value 10.0. You will see that the left hand side of the arithmetic assignment statement contains a single letter (often called a **variable**), but that the right hand side can contain several variables or numbers.

An arithmetic assignment statement is an instruction to the computer to work out the value of the right hand side, and give the single quantity on the left hand side that value. The following two statements have no meaning in FORTRAN.

P + C = A + B   A + B − C = Q

Any program containing them would be rejected and an error message printed out.

3.2 Powers of Numbers (Exponentiation)

5^2 and 2^3 are examples of powers of numbers. If you wish to calculate powers of numbers in a FORTRAN program, you write them like this: **5.0**2.0** or **2.0**3.0** or, more generally, you would have to write X^2 as **X**2.0** and P^3 as **P**3.0.** If, for example, **X** has the value 4.0 and **P** has the value 10.0, then the statement **Z** = **X**2.0** + **P**3.0** will give **Z** the value of 16.0 + 1000.0 or 1016.0.

Since the square root of a number can be written $X^{0.5}$ instead of $\sqrt{X}$, we may calculate the square root of a number in FORTRAN by writing **X**0.5** or even **X**(1.0/2.0).** If **R** has the value 2.0, then the statement **S** = **R**0.5** will assign the value 1.4142 to **S.**

Here are some examples of arithmetic assignment statements using **. **P** has the value 3.0.

R = 7.02.0**	This would give **R** the value 7.0 × 7.0 or 49.0
S = P0.5**	This would give **S** the value 1.732 (The square root of 3).
U = 2.0P**	This would give **U** the value 2.0 × 2.0 × 2.0 or 8.
T = 4.0*P2.0**	This would give **T** the value 4.0 × 9.0 or 36.0.

You will see that in the last of these examples the squaring is done before the multiplication by 4.0. This is an example of the general rule that in an arithmetic assignment statement—as in mathematics—raising a number to a power is always done first. If we wish to multiply **P** by 4.0 before squaring, we have to write the statement as **T = (4.0*P)**2;** which will give **T** the value 12.0 × 12.0 or 144.0.

3.3 Use of Brackets in FORTRAN

Sometimes in arithmetic and algebra you need to use brackets to make your meaning quite clear. Consider the two calculations 12 + 16 ÷ 2 and (12 + 16) ÷ 2. The value of the first is 12 + 8 or 20, and the value of the second is 28 ÷ 2 or 14.

In general, you can use brackets in FORTRAN in the same way as you use them in mathematics. If you are doubtful whether brackets are necessary in a particular case, put them in; your program will still work. If, for example, you wish to multiply two numbers and then divide by a third, you can make your meaning quite clear by writing **(P*Q)/R,** although in this particular case **P*Q/R** will give the same result.

Here are some examples of the use of brackets in FORTRAN. **P** and **Q** are given the values 12.0 and 4.0 respectively.

W = 2.0*Q + P	This will give **W** the value 8.0 + 12.0 or 20.0.
F = 2.0*(P + Q)	This will give **F** the value 2.0 × 16.0 or 32.0.
Z = P − (Q − 1.0)	This will give **Z** the value 12.0 − 3.0 or 9.0.
G = (P − Q) − 1.0	This will give **G** the value 8.0 − 1.0 or 7.0.

ASSIGNMENT 3.1

1. Given **X = 13.0, Y = 7.0,** and **Z = 10.0,** write down the value that will be assigned to the left hand side of each of these expressions.

a. **A = (X + Y)/Z**
b. **B = (X − Y)/(X + Y)**
c. **C = (X + Y)*Z**
d. **D = 2.0*X − 3.0*Y**
e. **E = X/2.0 + Z/4.0**
f. **F = (X + Y)*(Z*3.0 − 10.0)**
g. **G = − Z**
h. **H = X**2.0 + Y**2.0**

2. Rewrite these arithmetic assignment statements using the correct FORTRAN notation.

a. $U = X^3 - Y^3$
b. $V = (X - Y)^3$
c. $W = (A + B)/(A - B)$
d. $X = 23{,}457C^2$
e. $Y = \frac{1}{2}(T + B)H$
f. $Z = 4\pi R^3/3$

3.4 Mistakes in Arithmetic Assignment Statements

The most common mistakes are:

1. Writing real numbers without decimal points. For example, 2 instead of 2.0.
2. Using **I, J, K, L, M, N** to stand for real numbers.
3. Missing out * when doing multiplication.

It is also incorrect FORTRAN to have two signs such as a multiplication and a minus sign next to each other. The correct FORTRAN way of writing -2.0×-3.0 is **(− 2.0)*(− 3.0)** and the correct way of writing $5.0^{-2.0}$ is **5.0**(− 2.0)**.

ASSIGNMENT 3.2

Find the errors in the following arithmetic assignment statements.

1. **Z = 3*X + 4*Y**
2. **G = 4,456.4/Q**
3. **H = A(B + C)**
4. **F = S/2**
5. **X − Y = 3.0/Z**
6. **E = 6.0/M**

3.5 The Square Root Function

Instead of writing **X**0.5** to find the square root of **X,** it is more usual to write **SQRT(X),** so that if, for example, **X** has the value 81.0, the statement **Z = SQRT(X)** will give **Z** the value 9.0. This is an example of what is called a FORTRAN function; more examples of FORTRAN functions are given in Unit 12.

The variable in the bracket need not be a single letter. We could have, for example, **S = SQRT(B + C).** If **B** has the value 9.0 and **C** the value 40.0 then **S** will have the value 7.0. This is illustrated in Program 3.2, which calculates the longest side of a right-angled triangle given the two shortest sides, which we will call A and B.

The program has three main steps, which are shown on the flow chart. They are:

1. **Read** the values to be assigned to A and B.
2. **Calculate** the value of $\sqrt{A^2 + B^2}$ and assign this value to Z.
3. **Write** the value of Z.

You will see that in the flow chart we have inserted symbols containing **START** and **STOP.** These are standard symbols. Simple flow charts can be understood without them, but they are a help in understanding complicated flow charts. Therefore they are used in all the flow charts in the remainder of this book.

```
C       PROGRAM 3.2
        READ(2,1)A,B
      1 FORMAT(F5.1,F5.1)
        Z=SQRT(A**2.0+B**2.0)
        WRITE(3,2)Z
      2 FORMAT(1H ,F10.5)
        END
*DATA
   3.0   4.0
```

```
        5.00000
```

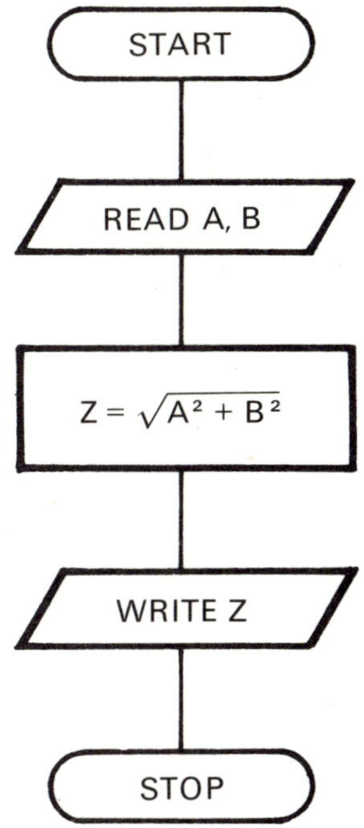

ASSIGNMENT 3.3

If **A** = **2.5** and **B** = **4.0,** what values will be assigned to the left hand side of each of these expressions?

1. **P = B**3.0**
2. **Q = 3.0**B**
3. **A = 2.0*A**
4. **S = (B + 5.0)/(B − 1.0)**
5. **X = A*B**2.0**
6. **X = (A*B)**2.0**
7. **Z = SQRT(B)**
8. **Y = (B + 1.0)**(B − 1.0)**
9. **U = 2.0*B**2.0 − 3.0*B + 7.0**
10. **R = (40.0*A)**0.5**

3.6 Finding Errors in Programs

There are two types of mistakes you can make in writing a program. The first type of mistake arises when FORTRAN is used incorrectly. For example, you may write **Z=A(B+C)** instead of **Z=A*(B+C)**. When the computer attempts to compile your program (that is translate it into machine language) it will be unable to do so and it will print out an error message. It will also do this for any other incorrect uses of FORTRAN. If you have made a mistake, you must correct your program, and the computer will compile it again. If there are no errors this time, the program can be executed and the computer will output the results.

These mistakes are not very serious, because the computer is almost sure to find them, although, of course, mistakes waste computer time and computer time is very expensive. We will not discuss this in detail, as each computer has its own set of error messages. When you have the chance to run your programs on a computer, you will soon find out what these error messages are.

The second type of mistake is more serious because the computer will not print out an error message. If, for example, you mean to write **Z = A + B**, but instead write **Z=A−B**, the computer will accept your program, but the answer you get will not, of course, be the answer you want. You must remember that the computer does exactly what you tell it to do, not what you meant to tell it to do.

The usual way of finding this sort of mistake is to test the program using numbers that you can easily check. In Program 3.1 we can see that 7.3 + 2.7 does come to 10.0, and in Program 3.2 we know that a right-angled triangle with the two shortest sides of length 3.0 and 4.0 has a longest side of length 5.0. We can see that these programs do what they are meant to do.

If you have to write a great many programs, you may find that you have to spend a considerable amount of time correcting and testing them. This is called **debugging** the programs; it often takes longer to debug a program than to write it.

ASSIGNMENT 3.4

1. Find the mistakes in this program, which is intended to calculate the square roots of 10.0 and 20.0. Write out the program correctly.

```
      X = SQRT(10)
      Y = SQRT(20)
      WRITE(3,1)X,Y,
      FORMAT(1H  ,F10.6,F10.6)
      END
*DATA
```

2. This program is intended to find the average of four numbers. Find the mistakes which it contains, and write out the program correctly.

```
      READ(2,10)P,Q,R,S
   10 FORMAT(F7.3,F7.3,F7.3,F7.3)
      A = P + Q + R + S/4.0
      WRITE(3,11)A
   11 FORMAT(1H ,F10.0)
      END
*DATA
```

3. Find the mistakes in this program, which is intended to find the area and circumference of a circle using the formulae $A = \pi R^2$ and $C = 2\pi R$. The letter **P** is used instead of π in the program. Write out the program correctly.

```
      READ(2,7)R
    7 FORMAT(F10.4)
      A = P*R**2.0
      B = 2.0*P*R
      WRITE(3,6)A,C
    6 FORMAT(1H ,F10.4,F10.4)
      END
*DATA
```

*3.7 The Order in which Operations are performed

When a computer comes to an arithmetic assignment statement, it does the arithmetic operations in the following order of priority:

1. raising number to **powers;**
2. the **multiplications and divisions;**
3. the **additions and subtractions.**

If, for example, a computer has to calculate:

3.0*2.04.0 + 4.5*2.0 − 7.0**

it first calculates

3.0*16.0 + 4.5*2.0 − 7.0

then

48.0 + 9.0 − 7.0

giving a final answer of

50.0.

Brackets can be used to depart from this order. If brackets are used, the order in which operations are performed can be varied.

If the computer has to calculate

(3.0 + 2.0)3.0**

it first calculates

5.03.0**

giving a final answer of

125.0

If the operations are of equal priority, the computer calculates from left to right. If, for example, a computer has to calculate

1.0 + 5.0 + 6.3

it first calculates

6.0 + 6.3

then the final answer of

12.3

ASSIGNMENT 3.5

1. Write a program to read the values of A, B, C, D and E, calculate (A + B + C)/(D + E) and print the answer.

2. Write a program to calculate the area between two concentric circles of given radii.

3. Write a program to calculate the surface area of a rectangular box, given its length width and height.

More about Calculations in FORTRAN

UNIT
4

4.1 Use of Names for Variables

So far in our arithmetic assignment statements we have used single letters for numbers. It is possible, however, to use names instead. For example, instead of writing **A** for area we may write **AREA,** and instead of **H** we may write **HEIGHT.** This is illustrated in Program 4.1, which calculates the area of a triangle using the formula:

$$AREA = \frac{1}{2} \times BASE \times HEIGHT$$

It is obviously very useful to be able to do this, as it makes the program easier to understand. It is also possible to use a mixture of letters and numbers to represent variables. For example, if you were writing a program to calculate the areas of two circles, the two areas could be called **A1** and **A2** or **AREA 1** and **AREA 2.**

So far our programs use only **REAL** numbers, that is numbers written with a decimal point. The names for the real variables in the program must obey the following rules:

1. The group must not contain more than **six** letters or numbers. (This may vary with some computers.)
2. The group must **not** start with a **number.**
3. The group must not start with the letters **I, J, K, L, M, N.**

For example, the following are not acceptable FORTRAN names for real variables:

CIRCUMFERENCE (More than six letters)
NUMBER (Starts with *N*)
5AREA (Starts with a number)

The following are acceptable:

VOLUME
CIRCUM
DIST6

```
C      PROGRAM 4.1
C      AREA OF TRIANGLE
       READ(2,1)BASE,HEIGHT
     1 FORMAT(F10.4,F10.4)
       AREA=0.5*BASE*HEIGHT
       WRITE(3,2)AREA
     2 FORMAT(1H ,F10.4)
       END
*DATA
    7.0         6.0
```

```
    21.0000
```

```
C       PROGRAM 4.2
C       AVERAGE OF FOUR NUMBERS
        READ(2,10)X1,X2,X3,X4
        AVE=(X1+X2+X3+X4)/4.0
        WRITE(3,20)AVE
   10   FORMAT(F10.4,F10.4,F10.4,F10.4)
   20   FORMAT(1H ,F10.4)
        END
*DATA
     3.0          6.0          7.0         1.0
```

```
      4.2500
```

Program 4.2 is another example of the use of names rather than single letters. It calculates the average of four real numbers.

You will see that in this program we have put the **FORMAT** statements at the end of the program. This is allowable, and is quite often done.

ASSIGNMENT 4.1

Which of the following are not acceptable FORTRAN names for real variables and why?

1. MEAN
2. VOLUME5
3. DIAM
4. 1STVOL
5. SUM
6. DIAMETER

4.2 How to shorten FORMAT Statements

If a program has to input or output a large quantity of numbers, it can be quite tedious writing out the **FORMAT** statements when these are very long. In FORTRAN the **FORMAT** statements can be shortened as in the following examples.

FORMAT(F10.4,F10.4,F10,4)
can be written **FORMAT(3F10.4)**
FORMAT(F10.4,F10.4,F6.1,F6.1)
can be written **FORMAT(2F10.4,2F6.1)**
FORMAT(1H ,F10.4,F5.2,F5.2,F10.4)
can be written **FORMAT(1H ,F10.4,2F5.2,F10.4)**

The shortened form of the **FORMAT** statement is used in Program 4.3, which inputs six real numbers and outputs them rounded up to the first decimal place.

```
C       PROGRAM 4.3
C       ROUNDING UP NUMBERS
        READ(2,7)A,B,C,D,E,F
    7   FORMAT(6F5.2)
        WRITE(3,5)A,B,C,D,E,F
    5   FORMAT(1H ,6F5.1)
        END
*DATA
 3.56 2.78 5.32 0.57-3.58 5.11
```

```
  3.6  2.8  5.3   .6 -3.6  5.1
```

ASSIGNMENT 4.2

1. Write these **FORMAT** statements in the shortened form.
   a. **FORMAT(1H ,F5.2,F5.2,F5.2)**
   b. **FORMAT(F6.3,F6.3,F10.4,F10.4,F10.4)**
   c. **FORMAT(1H ,F12.5,F16.7,F16.7,F10.4,F4.1,F4.1)**
2. Write a program to read a row of five real numbers and to print their square roots, also in a row. Use **F8.4** in your **FORMAT** statements.

Integer Numbers

UNIT
5

5.1 In writing our programs we have used only real numbers, that is numbers which are written with decimal points. There is another type of number which is used in computing, called an **INTEGER.** An integer is always a whole number, and it must not be written with a decimal point. Examples of integers are 25 and − 132. It is a good rule to use integers when the quantities which are being represented are whole numbers; for instance, the number of articles sold on a given day or someone's position in an examination.

You were told when you were learning about real numbers that you must never use the letters **I, J, K, L, M, N** to represent them. This is because these letters are reserved for integer variables.

5.2 The FORMAT Statements needed with INTEGERS

When you read and print integers, you must use a different type of **FORMAT** statement. If you were reading or writing a real number which had ten spaces reserved for it, with three figures after the point, you would have to write **F10.3.** If you were reading or writing an integer which had ten spaces reserved for it, you would need to put **I10** instead.

If you look at Program 5.1, you will see the points mentioned above in use. The program reads two integers and prints them in reverse order.
Again you will see that for both input and output, the numbers are placed on the right of the five spaces reserved for them, i.e. 13 must be spaced bbb13 and − 573 must be spaced b − 573

You are allowed to shorten **FORMAT** statements for integers in the same way that you are allowed to shorten them for real numbers.

For **FORMAT(I3,I10,I10,I10,I10)** we may write **FORMAT(I3,4I10)**
for **FORMAT(1H ,I8,I7,I7,I8)** we may write **FORMAT(1H ,I8,2I7,I8)**

```
C       PROGRAM 5.1
C       INPUT AND OUTPUT OF INTEGERS
        READ(2,5)J,K
      5 FORMAT(I5,I5)
        WRITE(3,6)K,J
      6 FORMAT(1H ,I5,I5)
        END
*DATA
   13 -573
```

```
  -573   13
```

```
C       PROGRAM 5.2
C       INPUT AND OUTPUT OF MIXED REAL AND INTEGER
        READ(2,7)A,M,B,N
      7 FORMAT(F5.1,I5,F5.1,I5)
        PROD=A*B
        I=M+N
        WRITE(3,8)PROD,I
      8 FORMAT(1H ,F8.2,I5)
        END
*DATA
   1.2    16   1.3    26
```

```
      1.56    42
```

It is possible to read or print a mixture of real and integer numbers provided that you use the correct **FORMAT** statement. This is illustrated in Program 5.2 which reads two integer and two real numbers, adds the integers, multiplies the real numbers, and prints the results.

The two types of number may be in any order provided that the order is the same in the **READ** statement, the **FORMAT** statement and the ***DATA.**

ASSIGNMENT 5.1

Write down FORMAT statements to go with each of the following **READ** or **WRITE** statements, using either **F5.1** or **I5** as necessary. For example, the **FORMAT** statement to go with **READ(2,9)K,A,B** should be **9 FORMAT(I5,2F5.1).**

1. **READ (2,4)A,B,K**
2. **WRITE (3,4)P,Q,R,N,M**
3. **READ (2,6)M,J,K,N,F**
4. **WRITE (3,9)D,H,K,N,L,R,E**

5.3 INTEGER Names

It is possible to use groups of letters or numbers to stand for the names of integers using the rules given in 4.1 Remember, though, that the group must start with one of the letters **I, J, K, L, M, N.**

The following are not acceptable:
AREA (Starts with **A**)
12N (Starts with a number)
NUMBER27 (More than six letters or digits)

The following are acceptable:
NUMBER **MEAN** **MEAN7**

ASSIGNMENT 5.2

Which of the following are not acceptable names for integer variables? Give your reasons.

1. **NUMERATOR**
2. **SUM**
3. **K45**
4. **2MEAN**
5. **MEAN2**
6. **IM51M**

5.4 INTEGERS in Arithmetic Assignment Statements

It is possible to use integers in arithmetic assignment statements. For example, if **I** and **J** have the values 5 and 8, then **M** = **I** + **J** will assign the value 13 to **M**. Most versions of FORTRAN do not allow the mixing of real and integer numbers in arithmetic assignment statements. For example, **M** = **I** + **3.0** is incorrect, but **M** = **I** + **3** is correct.

One important difference between the use of real and integer numbers in arithmetic assignment statements occurs in division. For example, if **I** and **N** have the values 23 and 5, then **M** = **I/N** will assign only the value 4 to **M** instead of 4.6. Similarly **N** = **4/6** will assign to **N** the value 0 instead of 0.66666. When two integers are divided, only the whole number part of the answer is given. This, as you will see later, has important uses in FORTRAN programs.

Here are some more examples of arithmetic assignment statements using integers. In these examples **I** has the value 45, **J** the value 9 and **K** the value 8.

M = **2*I**	gives **M** the value 90
N = **45/9**	gives **N** the value 5
I2 = **I/K**	gives **I2** the value 5 (The whole number part of 5.625)
L = **J**2**	gives **L** the value 81
MEAN = **(J + K)/2**	gives **MEAN** the value 8 (The whole number part of 8.5)

ASSIGNMENT 5.3

If **I** = **3**, **J** = **60**, **K** = **2**, what values are assigned to the left hand variables in the following expressions?

1. **M** = **I**K**
2. **N** = **(I + J)/2**
3. **L** = **K/I**
4. **M** = **(2*K)**I**
5. **M** = **2*(K**I)**
6. **L** = **6/5**
7. **L** = **5/6**
8. **N** = **I**2 + 4*I − 23**

Integers must not be used in **SQRT** functions. For example, **M** = **SQRT(9)** and **N** = **SQRT(I)** will both cause your program to be rejected.

Here are some incorrect arithmetic assignment statements, together with the corrections:

K = **3.0*J**	This should be **K** = **3*J**
M = **N**2.0 + L**2.0**	This should be **M** = **N**2 + L**2**

N = N*M*A	Real and integers mixed not allowed.
M = SQRT(L + J)	Integers not allowed in square root functions.

ASSIGNMENT 5.4

Write the correct version of the following arithmetic assignment statements. If it is impossible to write a correct version, say so.

1. I = L + 12.0

2. J = 1,467*M2**

3. S = 4*SQRT(4)

4. M = 15*K/B

5. N = 5.7*(K + L)

5.5 Mixing REAL and INTEGER Numbers

You have been told that in general you are not allowed to mix integer and real numbers in arithmetic assignment statements. There are two main exceptions to this rule.

1. The first exception is that if one side of an arithmetic assignment statement is real, then the other side may be integer. This is illustrated in the following examples, in which **G = 4.5, H = 6.0, M = 4, N = 3.**

K = 3.0*G	The value of the right hand side is 13.5. The computer takes the whole number part of this and gives **K** the value 13.
L = H/8.0	The value of the right hand side is $\frac{3}{4}$ or 0.75. The computer takes the whole number part of this and gives **L** the value 0.
J = G	The value of the right hand side of this is 4.5. The computer takes the whole number part of this and gives **J** the value 4.
D = M*N	The value of the right hand side is 12. **D** is a real number and takes the value 12.0.
S = M	The value of the right hand side is 4. **S** is a real number and takes the value 4.0.

Program 5.3 uses what you have just learned to calculate the remainder when one integer is divided by another.

When the computer comes to the line **I = M − (M/N)*N** it first calculates the value of **M/N,** which, in this case, comes to the whole number part of 26/8, which is 3. It then multiplies 3 by 8 to give 24, and subtracts this from 26 to give 2.

```
C      PROGRAM 5.3
C      CALCULATION OF REMAINDER WHEN M IS DIVIDED BY N
       READ(2,1)M,N
     1 FORMAT(2I10)
       I=M-(M/N)*N
       WRITE(3,2)I
     2 FORMAT(1H ,I10)
       END
*DATA
        26        8
```

```
         2
```

If you find this difficult to follow, read the following example, and then do the same thing with numbers that you choose yourself.
If **M** = **49** and **N** = **4**, then
I = **49** − **(49/4)*4** = **49** − **12*4** = **49** − **48** = **1**, which is, of course, the remainder when 49 is divided by 4.

Remember, the whole program is based on the fact that when one integer is divided by another the computer takes only the whole number part of the answer.

2. The second exception to the rule that you may not mix integer and real numbers in arithmetic assignment statements is that if you are taking powers of real numbers, you may write the exponent or power as an integer.

For example,
you may write **A****2.0** as **A****2**
you may write **15.36****4.0** as **15.36****4**

This only applies, of course, if the exponent is a whole number. For example, there is no way of writing **56.56****0.5**, by using integers. If you wish to use the fact that $56.56^{0.5} = 56.56^{1/2}$, you will have to write in in this way: **56.56****(1.0/2.0)**. Note that you may raise a real number to an integer power, but you cannot raise an integer to a real power.

The main advantage of writing exponents as integers where possible is that the computer then does this part of the calculation more rapidly.

ASSIGNMENT 5.5

Which of the following are incorrect FORTRAN?

1. **A = B**2**
2. **X = 3.5**2**
3. **N = M**3.0**
4. **X = 3.7**(1/3)**
5. **M = N**(1.0/2.0)**
6. **N = J**X**
7. **Y = X**J**
8. **A = (1/2)**3**

5.6 Changing the value of a variable in a Program

It is possible for a variable to change its value several times in a program. For example, the statement **N = N + 3** means that **N** takes the value of **N + 3.** If **N** was 7, then it will become 10. When a computer comes to an arithmetic assignment statement, it calculates the value of the right hand side and gives the variable on the left that value.

Here are some more examples. At the start of each example **M** has the value 10 and **Y** has the value 2.5.

M = 3*M	gives **M** the value 30.
M = M/M	gives **M** the value 1.
M = M + 15/M	gives **M** the value 11.
Y = SQRT(Y + 1.5)	gives **Y** the value 2.0.
Y = Y − Y	gives **Y** the value 0.0.

ASSIGNMENT 5.6

If **I = 6** and **J = 13,** what values will be assigned to the left hand side of each of the following expressions?

1. **I = J/I**
2. **I = (J/I)*I**
3. **I = (J*I)/I**
4. **J = (3*J + 2)/3**
5. **J = J + J/2**
6. **J = J − J**

ASSIGNMENT 5.7

1. Write a program to read an integer and to print out its square root.
2. Write a program to read five integers and to calculate and print out their average. (You will need to change from integers to real numbers somewhere in the program.)

Making Decisions in Programs

UNIT **6**

6.1 One of the most useful features of the computer is the ability to make decisions in the course of a calculation. The computer is programmed to do this by using **conditional statements.** A conditional statement is an instruction to the computer to take a certain course of action if a certain situation occurs. For example, a bank could programme its computer to print a letter to a customer if the customer's latest cheque made his account overdrawn.

So far the programs in this book have given the computer no choice in the way a calculation should be performed. They have given it a set of instructions, and there has been only one path through the program. If a program contains conditional statements, however, there will be more than one possible path.

6.2 The GREATER THAN Statement

We will first look at a simple program which reads a number and calculates 90% of that number if it is greater than 20; otherwise it calculates 95% of the number. Here is the flow chart for the program; you will see that the question *IS X GREATER THAN 20.0*? is placed inside a diamond-shaped box. This is called a **decision box.**

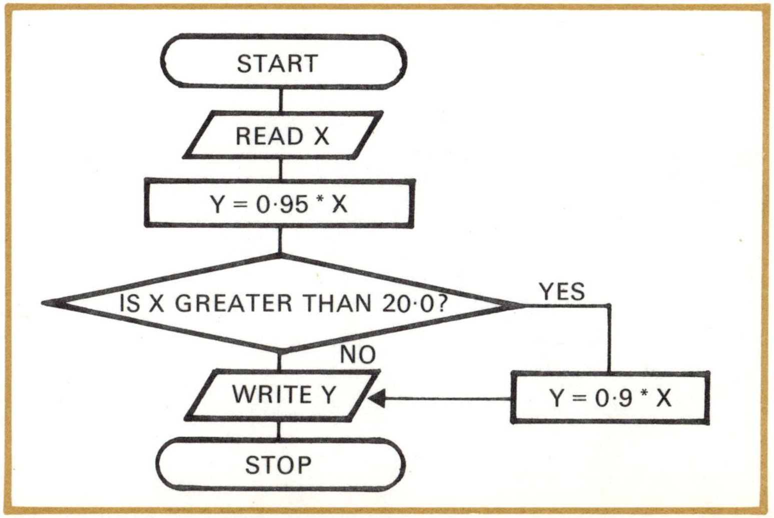


```
C     PROGRAM 6.1
C     EXAMPLE OF A CONDITIONAL STATEMENT
      READ(2,1)X
    1 FORMAT(F10.2)
      Y=0.95*X
      IF(X.GT.20.0)Y=0.9*X
      WRITE(3,2)Y
    2 FORMAT(1H ,F10.2)
      END
*DATA
    200.0
```

```
     180.00
```

After reading the number, the computer will calculate 95% of that number, whether it is greater than twenty or not. Then when it comes to the conditional statement **IF (X.GT.20.0)Y = 0.9*X** (the FORTRAN way of saying *If X is greater than* 20, *Y* = 90% *of X*), the computer will calculate a new value for **Y** only if **X** is greater than 20.0. If **X** is less than or equal to 20.0, then **Y** will retain its initial value. In program 6.1, since **X** is given the value 200.0, the computer will first assign the value of 190.0 to **Y** (95% of 200.0); but since **X** is greater than 20.0, the computer will then assign the new value of 180.0 to **Y** (90% of 200.0).

6.3 Other Conditional Statements

Other conditional statements are used in FORTRAN; the complete list is given below with examples of their use and meaning.

IF(X.LT.5.25)	If **X** is less than 5.25.
IF(K.LE.23)	If **K** is less than or equal to 23.
IF(N.EQ.K)	If **N** equals **K**.
IF(4.5.NE.Z)	If 4.5 is not equal to **Z**.
IF(67.GT.K)	If 67 is greater than **K**.
IF(A.GE.B)	If **A** is greater than or equal to **B**.

There are two important points to notice here. Firstly, the statement must contain two integer or two real quantities; a mixture such as IF(N.GE.6.5) is not allowed. Secondly, very careful attention must be paid to the use of the full stops and brackets. For example, the use of IF(R.GT 5.6) would lead to your program being rejected, as there is no full stop after GT.

ASSIGNMENT 6.1

1. If **N** and **X** have the values 5 and 2.5 at the start of each of these program segments, what will be the values of **M** or **Y** at the end of each segment?

a.
```
Y = 2.0*X
IF(N.EQ.7) Y = 3.0*X
```

b.
```
M = N**2
IF(X.LT.10.0) M = 2*N
```

c.
```
M = N**2
IF(M.EQ.25) M = 7
```

d.
```
IF(X.EQ.25.0) Y = 4.0*X
Y = 2.0*X
```

e.
```
Y = X + 1.0
IF(Y.GE.X) Y = X - 1.0
```

2. Find the errors in the following conditional statements. Write them out correctly.

a. **IF(X.LE.6)**

b. **IF(9.5.GE.M)**

c. **IF(M.EQN)**

6.4 Loops, GO TO and STOP Statements

Often a computer has to do a simple calculation hundreds or indeed thousands of times. In these cases the program can be made much shorter by using what is called a **loop.** A very simple example of a loop is shown in Program 6.2, which calculates the squares of the whole numbers from 1 to 5.

What the computer does in a loop is to repeat part of a program several times. In this particular case the value of a variable **N** is being increased by 1 each time to give it the values 1, 2, 3 and so on. **N** is assigned the value 0 by the statement **N = 0** at the beginning of the program. The computer then adds 1 to **N**, giving it the value 1, calculates the value of **N**2** and assigns this value to **M**. It prints the values of **N** and **M**. Since **N** is not at this stage equal to 5, the computer takes no notice of the conditional statement and goes on to the next statement, **GO TO 1.** The computer takes this as an instruction to return to the statement with the label 1 in front of it.

This statement now assigns the value 2 to **N**, and the next statement assigns the value 4 to **M**. These two values are then printed.

The computer goes through the loop 5 times; the fifth time through the loop, **N** has the value 5, the conditional statement is satisfied, and the computer will then **STOP** executing the program.

You should notice that ***DATA** is used, although, in fact, there is no data to be read. This is necessary with the computer we are using to process the programs in this book; with some computers, however, ***DATA** is not needed in the program.

The arrow shown on the listing is not, of course, produced by the computer, but has been added later to make the program easier for you to follow.

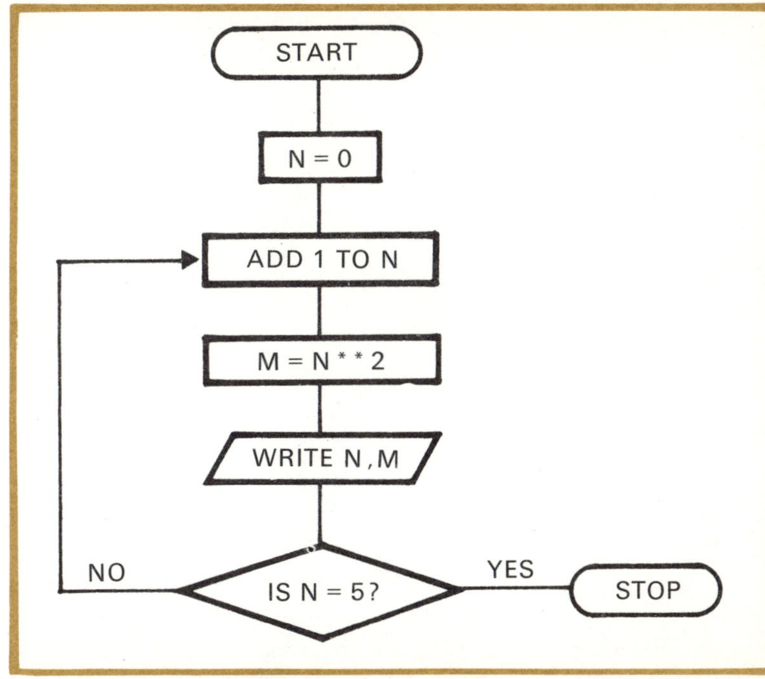


```
C       PROGRAM 6.2
C       EXAMPLE OF A LOOP
        N=0
      1 N=N+1
        M=N**2
        WRITE(3,2)N,M
      2 FORMAT(1H ,2I5)
        IF(N.EQ.5)STOP
        GO TO 1
        END
*DATA
```

```
    1    1
    2    4
    3    9
    4   16
    5   25
```

ASSIGNMENT 6.2

1. What would happen if the statement **IF (N.EQ.5) STOP** had not been included in program 6.2?
2. Show the changes necessary so that Program 6.2 would output:—
   (*a*) The squares of the numbers from 1 to 20.
   (*b*) The cubes of the numbers from 100 to 200.
   (*c*) The cubes of the even numbers from 100 to 200.
   (*d*) The cubes of the even numbers from 200 down to 100.

3. Write down the output of the following program.

```
      N = 42
    1 N = N - 2
      I = N/2
      WRITE(3,2)I
    2 FORMAT(1H ,I5)
      IF(N.EQ.18) STOP
      GO TO 1
      END
*DATA
```

6.5 The use of a Loop in a Data Processing problem

Many computers are used in business where they are often required to do a large number of simple calculations. Work of this type is often called **data processing.** Examples of data processing are: valuing the stocks of a shop or factory; keeping a check on overdue books in a large library; and keeping income tax records. A typical data processing problem is that of sorting through a list of numbers and printing out those that satisfy a certain condition. For example, from a long list of numbers we may wish to select those greater than 100.0. Program 6.3 does this for a sequence of five numbers.

This program is designed to deal with a sequence of numbers of any length; merely by inputting the necessary data, we could use it just as readily for thousands of numbers. To make this possible the data must terminate with what is called a **stop number.** In our example any number larger than 9000.0 will act as a stop number; we have used 9999.0. As the computer reads each number, it examines it to see if it is greater than 9000,0; if it is, then the computer will stop executing the program. Remember that the stop number must be larger than any number that we are likely to use with our program; otherwise the program will stop too soon.

When the computer reads the first number it assigns the value 73.59 to **X**. Since this value of **X** is not greater than 9000.0 the computer proceeds to the next conditional statement. Since **X** is less than 100.0, the computer returns to the **READ** statement. The computer does nothing with this value of **X**.

```
C       PROGRAM 6.3
C       NUMBER SORTING
      1 READ(2,2)X
      2 FORMAT(F10.4)
        IF(X.GT.9000.0)STOP
        IF(X.LE.100.0)GO TO 1
        WRITE(3,4)X
      4 FORMAT(1H ,F10.4)
        GO TO 1
        END
*DATA
    73.59
  4584.973
     4.4567
   101.0
  9999.0
```

```
  4584.9730
   101.0000
```

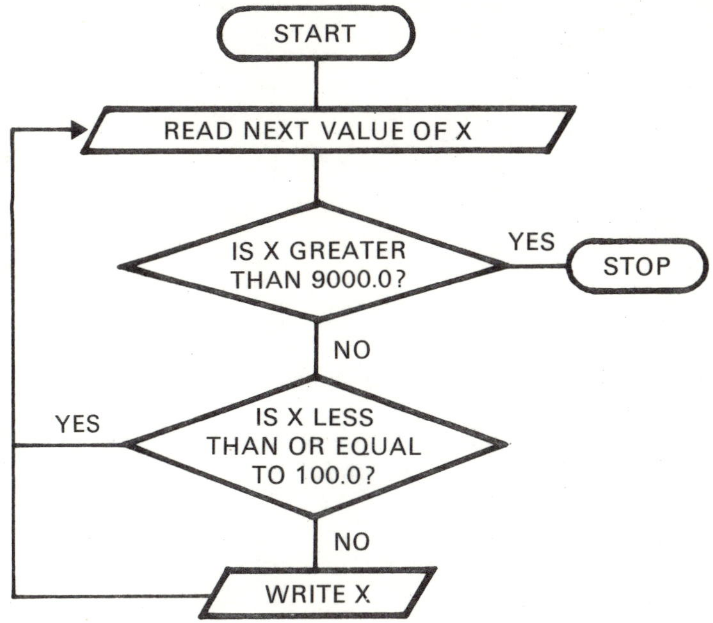

When the computer returns to the **READ** statement it reads the next number and assigns to **X** the value 4584.973. It again ignores the next conditional statement; but when it comes to **IF(X.LE.100.0) GO TO 1,** it will not jump back to 1, but will continue with the next instruction and will print the value of **X.** It will then jump back to 1.

The next two numbers are dealt with in the same way, but when it comes to the fifth number, **X** is assigned the value 9999.0 and the first conditional statement will cause the computer to stop executing the program. You will see that each item of data is given a separate line. This layout is necessary because each time the computer goes through the loop and reads the next value of **X,** it has to use the **FORMAT** statement again; and each time a **FORMAT** statement is used, the computer will go to the next line of data, or the next card.

You should remember that the stop number is not one of the numbers that you intend to be sorted, but is an extra one placed at the end to tell the computer that there are no more numbers to be dealt with.

ASSIGNMENT 6.3

1. Show the alterations that you would make to Program 6.3 so that it would:

(*a*) Output the numbers less than 50.0.

(*b*) Output the numbers greater than 70.0, excluding of course the stop number.

(*c*) Output the numbers from 100.0 to 200.0 inclusive. You will need to add an extra conditional statement.

2. Write down the output of Program 6.3 if the second conditional statement was changed to:

a. **IF(X.EQ.101.0) GO TO 1**

b. **IF(X.NE.73.59) GO TO 1**

c. **IF(X.NE.100.0) GO TO 1**

3. Write down the output of the following program:

```
      1 READ(2,2)N
      2 FORMAT(I5)
        IF(N.EQ.1000) STOP
        IF(N.GT.20) GO TO 1
        WRITE(3,3)N
      3 FORMAT(1H ,I5)
        GO TO 1
        END
*DATA
     21
     19
     36
     45
      2
   1000
```

ASSIGNMENT 6.4

1. Write a program to output a table of the squares and square roots of the whole numbers from 100 to 120.

2. Write a program to input a sequence of 100 numbers and to output those which are negative.

3. Write a program to input the co-ordinates of ten points and to output those which are less than five units from the origin.

The use of DO Loops

UNIT 7

7.1 In Unit 6 you were introduced to loops which were used to repeat a series of similar calculations several times. These loops are so important that most computing languages make special provision for putting loops into programs rather more easily than we did in Unit 6. In FORTRAN these simplified loops are called **DO loops** or **DO statements.**

Program 7.1, which calculates the squares of the whole numbers from 1 to 5, is similar to Program 6.2. If you compare the two programs, you will see that a **DO** statement makes the flow chart and the program shorter, and easier to write.

```
C       PROGRAM 7.1
C       EXAMPLE OF A DO LOOP
        DO 7 N=1,5
        M=N**2
        WRITE(3,2)N,M
      2 FORMAT(1H ,2I5)
      7 CONTINUE
        END
*DATA
```

```
    1    1
    2    4
    3    9
    4   16
    5   25
```

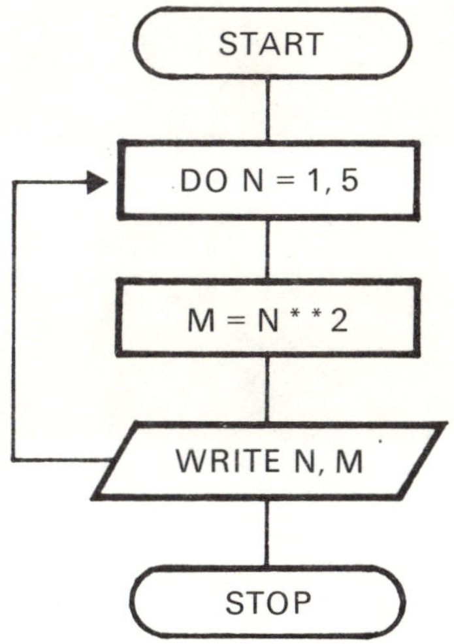

```
C       PROGRAM 7.2
  ┌────>DO 7 N=5,10,2
  │     I=N**2
  │     WRITE(3,5)N,I
  │   5 FORMAT(1H ,2I5)
  └───7 CONTINUE
        END
*DATA
```

```
    5   25
    7   49
    9   81
```

When the computer comes to **DO 7 N = 1,5,** it takes this as an instruction to perform the section of the program down to **7 CONTINUE; N** is equal to 1 the first time, 2 the second time, and so on. For example, the third time through the loop, **N** is assigned the value 3, **M** is assigned the value 9, and these two values are then output.

The 7 in the **DO** statement has no particular significance; it could just as well be any other integer, provided that the same integer is used for the statement number in front of **CONTINUE.**

If we needed to print the squares of the whole numbers from say 300 to 350, we could do this by changing the **DO** statement to **DO 7 N = 300,350.**

It is sometimes helpful, particularly with long programs, to insert an arrow going from CONTINUE to the start of the loop just as in the flow chart, although you take no notice of it when you punch the program.

You will see that in Program 7.1 the values of **N** jump by 1 every time the computer goes through the **DO** loop. If we wish it to jump by 2 instead, we have to write the **DO** statement with a 2 at the end of it, as in Program 7.2.

The first time through the **DO** loop, **N** will have the value 5, the second time the value 7, the third time the value 9. The next value of **N** would have been 11, but this is more than 10 and so the computer will stop calculating. You would get exactly the same results if you put **DO 7 N = 5,9,2** instead.

All the numbers in **DO** statements must be integers, never real numbers or 0. The letters used must be either **I, J, K, L, M** or **N.** For example, **DO 8 L = 50,100,7** is an acceptable **DO** statement.

DO 9 M = 12.0,16.0,0.5 is not an acceptable **DO** statement because it contains real numbers.

And **DO 1 I = 0,100** is not acceptable because it contains **0.**

ASSIGNMENT 7.1

1. What would Program 7.1 print out if the **DO** statement was **DO 7 N = 1,3 ?**
2. What would it print out if the **DO** statement was **DO 7 N = 4,13,3 ?**
3. What would it print out if the **DO** statement was **DO 7 N = 4,15,3 ?**

4. What would this program print out?

```
        DO 12 K = 10,20,3
        J = K + 6
        WRITE(3,1)K,J
      1 FORMAT(1H  ,2I5)
     12 CONTINUE
        END
*DATA
```

5. Write a program to calculate the cubes of the numbers from 2 to 5. The numbers are to be printed together with their cubes, as in Program 7.1.

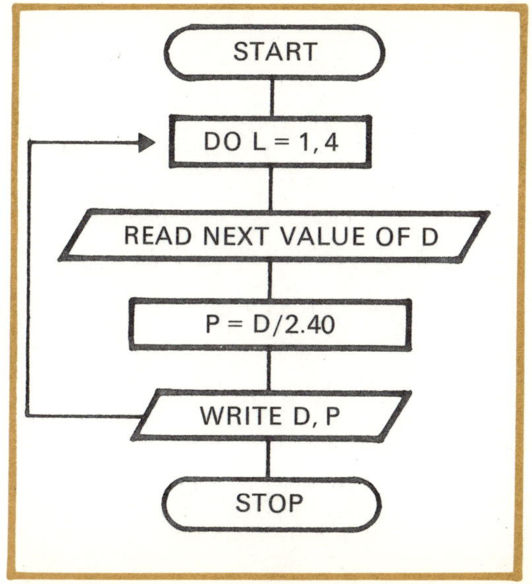

7.2 An Example of the DO Statement in Data Processing

Program 7.3 uses a **DO** loop to read a column of prices in dollars, to convert these prices to pounds, and to print the prices in both pounds and dollars. Both currencies are written in decimal form, and it is assumed that one pound equals 2.40 dollars.

The computer will go through the **DO** loop four times, with **L** equal to 1 the first time, 2 the second and so on. You will see that the value of **L** is not actually used in the program; its purpose is to act as a counter so that the computer carries out a series of instructions four times.

The first time through the loop, the computer will read in the first value in the data and divide by 2.40 to change to pounds. It will then print out the amount in dollars followed by the amount in pounds. The second time through the loop, the computer will read the second value in the data, and so on. If we needed to deal with 400 numbers instead of 4, we would just need to replace the 4 in the **DO** statement by 400.

```
C       PROGRAM 7.3
C       CHANGING DOLLARS TO POUNDS
        DO 1 L=1,4
        READ(2,2)D
      2 FORMAT(F10.2)
        P=D/2.40
        WRITE(3,4)D,P
      4 FORMAT(1H ,2F10.4)
      1 CONTINUE
        END
*DATA
     13.50
    450.0
     12.66
     48.0
```

```
   13.5000     5.6250
  450.0000   187.5000
   12.6600     5.2750
   48.0000    20.0000
```

ASSIGNMENT 7.2

1. Write a program to read in five numbers and to print each number followed by its square root.

2. Write down the output of the following program.

```
      DO 3 M = 1,5
      READ(2,1)X,Y
      Z = X + Y
      WRITE(3,2)Z
    3 CONTINUE
    1 FORMAT(2F5.1)
    2 FORMAT(1H ,F5.1)
      END
*DATA
  5.2  4.3
  4.9  4.3
  4.3 -4.3
 -3.7  5.7
  0.0  4.0
```

7.3 Producing REAL Numbers with a DO Statement

If we wish to produce a table of the square roots of the numbers from say 10 to 15, it is not possible to do this just with a **DO** loop. The **DO** loop can produce only the integers from 10 to 15, and we cannot find the square root of an integer in FORTRAN. We need some method of producing the real numbers from 10.0 to 15.0. Program 7.4 shows how this is done.

```
C     PROGRAM 7.4
C     SQUARE ROOTS OF NUMBERS FROM 10 TO 15
      DO 1 L=10,15
      X=L
      S=SQRT(X)
      WRITE(3,11)L,S
   11 FORMAT(1H ,I3,F7.4)
    1 CONTINUE
      END
*DATA
```

```
 10 3.1623
 11 3.3166
 12 3.4641
 13 3.6056
 14 3.7417
 15 3.8730
```

The first time through the loop, **L** has the value 10, **X** is a **REAL** number with the value 10.0, and the value of **S** is 3.1623. The second time through the loop, **L** has the value 11, **X** takes the value 11.0, **S** is given the value 3.3166 and so on. The important step to remember is the line **X** = **L**, which changes an **INTEGER** number to a **REAL** number so that we can use the **SQRT** function.

7.4 Producing Decimal Numbers with DO Statements

Sometimes it is necessary to produce a set of real decimal numbers. This can also be done using a **DO** loop. Program 7.5 produces and outputs the numbers from 6.1 to 6.7 by steps of 0.1.

The first time through the loop, **N** takes the value 61. The purpose of the line **X** = **N** is to change 61 from integer to real. If this line was left out the next line would be **Y** = **N/10.** This would not give **Y** the value 6.1 but the value 6.0 as explained in Unit 5. After the integer 61 has been converted to the real number 61.0, however, the line **Y** = **X/10** will assign the value 6.1 to **Y**.

The next time through the loop, **N** takes the value 62, **X** takes the value 62.0 and **Y** takes the value 6.2, and so on.

```
C      PROGRAM 7.5
C      PRODUCING DECIMALS WITH A DO LOOP
       DO 4 N=61,67
       X=N
       Y=X/10.0
       WRITE(3,5)Y
     5 FORMAT(1H ,F4.1)
     4 CONTINUE
       END
*DATA
```

```
  6.1
  6.2
  6.3
  6.4
  6.5
  6.6
  6.7
```

ASSIGNMENT 7.3

1. Write a program to print the numbers 5.1, 5.2, ... 6.0 together with their square roots. Have the output in two columns, with the square roots in the right hand column.
2. Write a program to read a column of five integers, change each one to a real number, multiply each number by 1.1, and print the new values in column form.
3. Write a program to print the numbers from − 1.1 to − 1.9 by steps of 0.1 (Hint: If, for example, **X** = **7.0,** then **Y** = − **X** will give **Y** the value − **7.0**)

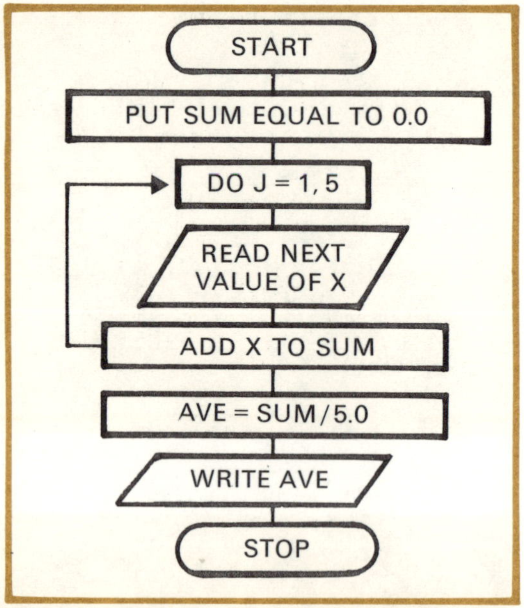


```
C       PROGRAM 7.6
C       AVERAGE OF FIVE NUMBERS
        SUM=0.0
        DO 1 J=1,5
        READ(2,2)X
      2 FORMAT(F6.2)
        SUM=SUM+X
      1 CONTINUE
        AVE=SUM/5.0
        WRITE(3,3)AVE
      3 FORMAT(1H ,F6.2)
        END
*DATA
 12.0
  7.0
  5.0
  4.0
 10.0
```

```
    7.60
```

4. Write down the output of this program.

```
      DO 1 J = 1,5
      READ(2,2)M,N
    2 FORMAT(2I5)
      X = M
      Y = N
      Z = X/Y
      WRITE(3,3)Z
    3 FORMAT(1H ,F10.4)
    1 CONTINUE
      END
*DATA
    4    2
    5    1
   -5   -5
    8    6
    3    6
```

7.5 The Average of a series of numbers using a DO Statement

It is often necessary to read a series of numbers and add them together. This would be the first step, for instance, in finding an average. If you look at Program 7.6, you will see how the average of five numbers is calculated. A change in the **DO** statement will enable the program to deal with any set of numbers.

You will find the program easy to understand if you look at the flow chart first. The first thing that happens is that **SUM** is given the value 0.0. The first time through the loop, the first value of **X** is read and added to **SUM**, which now has the value 12.0. The second time through the loop, the second value of **X** is read and added to **SUM**, which now has the value 19.0. This is repeated three more times to give **SUM** the final value 38.0. The important thing to remember here is that **SUM** must be given the value 0.0 to start with.

The computer now leaves the **DO** loop, calculates the value of 38.0/5.0 and prints the answer.

ASSIGNMENT 7.4

1. Rewrite program 7.6 so that it prints the product of the five numbers instead of their average.

2. Rewrite program 7.6 so that it prints the sum of the squares of the numbers.

*3. Rewrite Program 7.6 so that it prints the "average" of the first number, then the average of the first two, then the average of the first three and so on.

7.6 Another Example of a DO Statement used in Data Processing

The table below shows the numbers of various items sold by a shop in each of the twelve months of the year. We are going to write a program to calculate the total number of each item sold in the year.

	January	February	March	April	May	June	July	August	September	October	November	December
CHAIRS	12	13	17	5	6	6	7	13	10	8	7	5
CUPBOARDS	4	7	8	4	6	7	9	1	3	5	6	4
ARMCHAIRS	4	6	8	4	6	7	9	2	10	12	4	6
SETTEES	1	0	2	3	2	1	3	4	2	1	0	2
TABLES	6	8	5	9	6	7	5	7	8	9	5	3

We will start by writing a flow chart. The steps we need to include are:
1. Read the first row.
2. Total the first row.
3. Print the first total.
4. Read the second row, and so on.

This will give us the following flow chart:

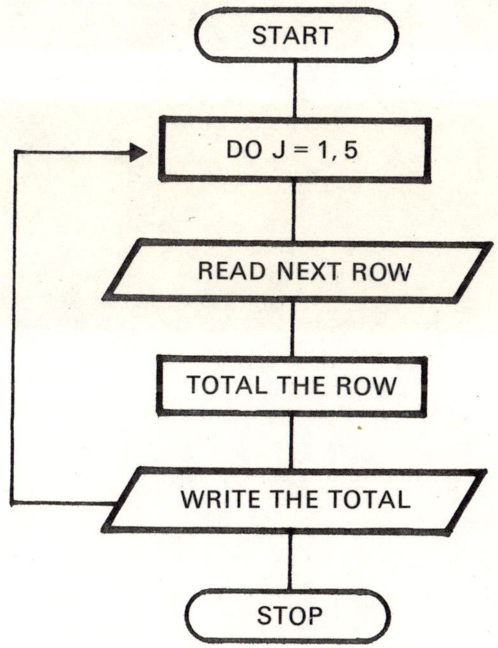

The first time through the loop, the computer will read the twelve values on the first line, add them, assign the value 109 to **M**, and output the value of **M**. The second time through the loop, it will read the values on the second line, and so on. This is not in fact the best way of writing this particular program. A program like this is usually written using **arrays**, which are dealt with in Unit 9.

```
C       PROGRAM 7.7
        DO 1 J=1,5
        READ(2,2)N1,N2,N3,N4,N5,N6,N7,N8,N9,N10,N11,N12
      2 FORMAT(12I3)
        M=N1+N2+N3+N4+N5+N6+N7+N8+N9+N10+N11+N12
        WRITE(3,3)M
      3 FORMAT(1H ,I5)
      1 CONTINUE
        END
*DATA
 12 13 17  5  6  6  7 13 10  8  7  5
  4  7  8  4  6  7  9  1  3  5  6  4
  4  6  8  4  6  7  9  2 10 12  4  6
  1  0  2  3  2  1  3  4  2  1  0  2
  6  8  5  9  6  7  5  7  8  9  5  3
```

```
  109
   64
   78
   21
   78
```

ASSIGNMENT 7.5

1. What alteration is needed to Program 7.7 to enable it to read ten rows?
2. What alteration is needed to Program 7.7 to enable it to calculate and print the average number of each item sold per month?
3. What alteration would be needed to Program 7.7 to enable it to calculate the total of all the items sold in the year?
4. What alteration is needed to Program 7.7 to enable it to print the total numbers of each item sold in the first six months?

5. Write a program to print the sum of the products of the two columns below. i.e. to calculate 7 × 5 + 3 × 2 + . . .

7	5
3	2
1	7
6	9
3	0
4	7
5	9

7.7 An Example of a Conditional Statement in a DO Loop

We will now consider the program that a bank might use if it wanted to find the total of all the accounts that were in credit, ignoring the accounts which were overdrawn. Program 7.8 does this for eight accounts; only a change in the size of the **DO** loop is needed to make the program capable of processing any number of accounts.

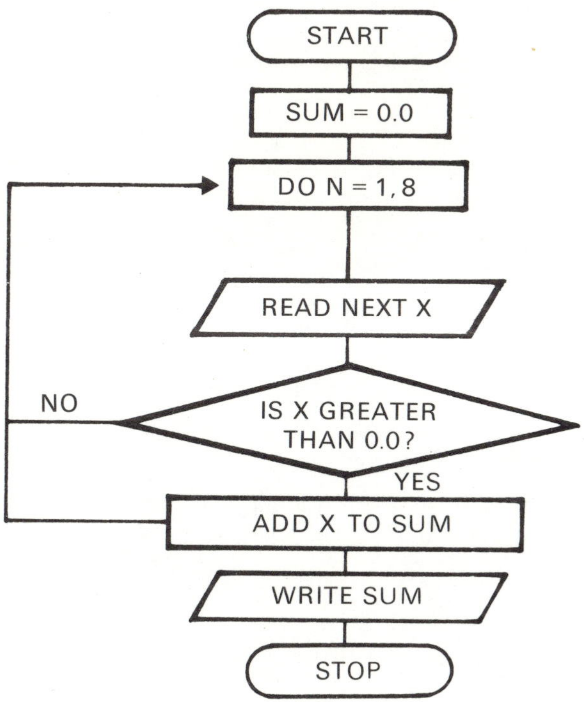


```
C       PROGRAM 7.8
C       THE SUM OF THE POSITIVE MEMBERS
C       OF A SET OF NUMBERS
        SUM=0.0
        DO 3 N=1,8
        READ(2,1)X
      1 FORMAT(F10.2)
        IF(X.GT.0.0)SUM=SUM+X
      3 CONTINUE
        WRITE(3,4)SUM
      4 FORMAT(1H ,F10.4)
        END
*DATA
       13.1
      -46.23
       12.6
      -45.5
      -36.78
      -58.98
       13.0
      100.0
```

```
    138.7000
```

The first time through the **DO** loop, **X** is greater than 0.0, so **SUM** becomes 0.0 + 13.1, or 13.1 The second time through the loop, **X** is less than 0.0, and so **SUM** keeps the value 13.1. The third time through the loop, **X** is greater than 0.0 and **SUM** becomes 13.1 + 12.6 or 25.7; this process continues, giving a final value for **SUM** of 138.7. It is important to note that the value of **X** is added to **SUM** only if **X** is greater than 0.0.

7.8 DO Loops of variable size

So far all the **DO** loops that we have used have covered a fixed range of numbers. But sometimes we require a different range of numbers each time the program is executed. For example, we might require **DO 1 J = 10,20,2** on one occasion and **DO 1 J = 40,80,5** on another. This problem can be overcome by writing **DO 1 J = I,M,N** and then inputting the values of **I,M,N** that we wish to use with the data.

This is demonstrated in Program 7.9 which, with the given data, calculates the squares of the even numbers from 20 to 30. After the values to be assigned to **I,M,N,** have been input, the **DO** statement becomes **DO 1 J = 20,30,2.** If we wished to produce a table of squares of the multiples of five from, say, 25 to 95, we would need to provide 25; 95; 5 as data.

If you compare this program with Program 7.2, you will see that this time, by using the letters **I,M,N** instead of particular numbers in the **DO** statement, we can use our program unchanged for any sequence of numbers we wish; all we need do is supply the required data.

```
C        PROGRAM 7.9
         READ(2,3)I,M,N
       3 FORMAT(3I5)
         DO 1 J=I,M,N
         L=J**2
         WRITE(3,2)L
       2 FORMAT(1H ,I10)
       1 CONTINUE
         END
*DATA
   20   30    2
```

```
         400
         484
         576
         676
         784
         900
```

ASSIGNMENT 7.6

1. What data would be needed in Program 7.9 so that it would print out the squares of the odd numbers from 3 to 17?

2. What would the output of Program 7.9 be if the numbers 21,49,7 were read in?

3. What would the output of Program 7.9 be if the numbers 36,70,12 were read in?

ASSIGNMENT 7.7

1. Write a program to read a series of 20 numbers and print the square roots of the non-negative numbers.

2. Write a program to calculate the average of the members of a sequence of numbers. The number of members in the sequence will be read in with the sequence.

3. Write a program to calculate the average of the squares of a sequence of numbers, reading in the size of the sequence with the sequence.

***4.** Write programs similar to those in 2 and 3, but with the data terminating with a stop number. If a **DO** loop is used it can be of fixed size, but should be large encough to deal with any likely sequence.

***5.** Write a program similar to Program 7.8, but adapt it to print the total of the overdrafts as well. You will need a second conditional statement and you will have to keep two sums; you can call them for example **SUM1** and **SUM2**.

UNIT
8

More advanced use of FORMAT Statements—

8.1 Input and Output of more than one line with a single FORMAT Statement

It is often necessary to input or output more data than can be fitted into the space available on one line, usually 72 spaces or print positions. We may wish, for example, to input twelve numbers, each one occupying seven spaces. It is impossible to input these on a single line (or card) as this will require 84 spaces. We could, however, do it as follows:

```
      READ(2,1)A,B,C,D,E,F
      READ(2,2)G,H,P,Q,R,S
    1 FORMAT(6F7.2)
    2 FORMAT(6F7.2)
*DATA
   1.1    1.2    1.3    1.4    1.5    1.6
   1.7    1.8    1.9    2.0    2.1    2.2
```

It is possible to read in these twelve numbers using just one **READ** statement and one **FORMAT** statement. This is done in the program segment 8.1, for which the data would be arranged as above.

```
  PROGRAM 8.1
  READ(2,1)A,B,C,D,E,F,G,H,P,Q,R,S
1 FORMAT(6F7.2)
```

The **READ** statement tells the computer that it has to read twelve numbers. When the computer has read **A,B,C,D,E,F,** it 'runs out' of **FORMAT** statement, which has allowed for only six numbers. When this happens, the computer returns to the start of the **FORMAT** statement and uses it again, at the same time jumping to the start of the next line of data (or to the next card if punched cards are being used).

If at some stage in the program we wish to print out these twelve numbers in the same two rows, the instruction will be:

```
  WRITE(3,5)A,B,C,D,E,F,G,H,P,Q,R,S
5 FORMAT(1H ,6F7.2)
```

When the computer has printed out six numbers, the **FORMAT** statement has been 'used up', and the computer will return to the start of the

FORMAT statement. The **1H** at the start of the statement will instruct the printer to start printing out the next six numbers on a new line.

Here are some more examples:

1.
```
      READ(2,1)U,V,W,X,Y,Z
    1 FORMAT(2F4.1)
```
would read in
```
*DATA
  5.6 4.9
  7.3 3.5
  3.6 2.8
```
(Here the **FORMAT** statement is being used three times.)

and
```
      WRITE(3,4)U,V,W,X,Y,Z
    4 FORMAT(1H ,3F5.2)
```
would write out
```
  5.6  4.9  7.3
  3.5  3.6  2.8
```

2.
```
      READ(2,7)I1,I2,I3,I4
    7 FORMAT(2I5)
```
would read in
```
*DATA
     73  456
    -57   78
```
and
```
      WRITE(3,8)I1,I2,I3,I4
    8 FORMAT(1H ,I5)
```
would write out
```
   73
  456
  -57
   78
```

3.
```
      READ(2,9)A,B,I,X,Y,J
    9 FORMAT(2F5.1,I5)
```
would read in
```
*DATA
    2.5  6.7    9
    6.8 23.9   67
```
and
```
      WRITE(3,5)A,I,B,X,J,Y
    5 FORMAT(1H ,F5.1,I5,F5.1)
```
would write out
```
  2.5    9   6.7
  6.8   67  23.9
```

4. The following segment of program will read in only those values shown in the box.

```
          READ(2,1)A,B,C,D,E,F,G
        1 FORMAT(3F4.1)
*DATA
 4.5 6.7 4.3 3.7 4.7
 2.6 4.8 5.4 3.8 2.7
 2.8 6.4 6.9 4.7 6.9
```

In the same way as in Program 8.1, the **FORMAT** statement instructs the computer to read the first three numbers of the data and then jumps to the start of the next line of the data (or to the next card). As before, it reads the next three numbers and again jumps to the start of the next line. As the **READ** statement now leaves only the value of **G** to be read, the computer reads the first number on the third line. In this way, for example, **D** will be assigned the value 2.6 and **G** the value 2.8.

ASSIGNMENT 8.1

1. Rewrite the **FORMAT** statement in the segment labelled Program 8.1 so that it will read data arranged as follows. (Blank spaces are indicated by b)

a.
```
bb1.1bb1.2
   1.3   1.4
   1.5   1.6
   1.7   1.8
   1.9   2.0
   2.1   2.2
```

b.
```
bb1.1bb1.2bb1.3bb1.4
   1.5   1.6   1.7   1.8
   1.9   2.0   2.1   2.2
```

c.
```
bb1.1bb1.2bb1.3bb1.4bb1.5
   1.6   1.7   1.8   1.9   2.0
   2.1   2.2
```

2. If **N1** = **1**; **N2** = **2**; **N3** = **3** and so on, write down the output of the following program segment:

```
WRITE (3,1)N1,N2,N3,N4,N5,N6
```

if these **FORMAT** statements are used.

a. FORMAT(1H ,3I2)
b. FORMAT(1H ,2I2)
c. FORMAT(1H ,I2)
d. FORMAT(1H ,4I2)
e. FORMAT(1H ,8I2)

8.2 The use of / in Input and Output

If we wish the computer to read or print a line of integers, followed by a line of real numbers, followed by a line containing both integers and real numbers, we cannot use the method of the previous section. That method works only if the same **FORMAT** statement can be used for each line. Program segment 8.2 inputs the three lines described, but you will see that it is rather long.

```
        PROGRAM 8.2
        READ(2,1)I,J
        READ(2,2)A,B
        READ(2,3)K,C
      1 FORMAT(2I5)
      2 FORMAT(2F5.1)
      3 FORMAT(I5,F5.1)
*DATA
   45   76
 52.4  2.9
  343  5.9
```

A program segment of this type can be made much shorter by the use of the slash, /, in the **FORMAT** statement. The effect of the slash in a **FORMAT** statement is to tell the computer to start a new line of output or input. Program 8.3 has the same effect as Program 8.2, but has been made considerably shorter by the use of the slash.

The computer reads the values of **I** and **J** using the **2I5** in the **FORMAT** statement, but it then comes to /, which instructs it to start reading from the next line (or card).

```
        PROGRAM 8.3
        READ(2,1)I,J,A,B,K,C
      1 FORMAT(2I5/2F5.1/I5,F5.1)
*DATA
   45   76
 52.4  2.9
  343  5.9
```

If we wish to print these numbers in the same three rows, we need the following instructions:

```
  WRITE(3,7)I,J,A,B,K,C
7 FORMAT(1H  ,2I5/1H  ,2F5.1/1H  ,I5,F5.1)
```

Note that on output, / must be followed by **1H ,**.

Here is another example of the use of the slash.

```
      READ(2,1)A,B,C,D,E,I
    1 FORMAT(3F6.2/2F5.1/I3)
```

would read in

```
*DATA
   5.3    5.43   6.57
   6.5   5.7
  45
```

and

```
        WRITE(3,8)I,A,B,C,D,E
     8  FORMAT(1H ,I5,2F10.4/1H ,3F6.2)
```

would print out

```
   45      5.3           5.43
  6.57   6.5     5.7
```

ASSIGNMENT 8.2

1. Complete the **FORMAT** statements of these program segments:

a.

```
          READ(2,15)I,J,K,L,M
     15   FORMAT
 *DATA
     56   787
     34    67     89
```

b.

```
          READ(2,4)A,J,K,C
      4   FORMAT
 *DATA
    5.9  4567
  -4597  24.0
```

c.

```
          READ(2,7)A,B,C,L,M,N
      7   FORMAT
 *DATA
   5.57  4.89-3.69
  -4565  3458  4536
```

d.

```
          READ(2,1)K1,K2,K3,K4
      1   FORMAT
 *DATA
   3456
  -6785
    679  5709
```

2. Write down the output of these program segments, using the values given to the variables in *b* and *d* above:

a.

```
     WRITE(3,1)A,C,J,K
   1 FORMAT(1H ,2F5.1/1H ,2I5)
```

b.

```
     WRITE(3,2)K1,K2,K3,K4
   5 FORMAT(1H ,3I5/1H ,I15)
```

8.3 Continuation Lines

The standard coding form contains 72 spaces in a line. If you need to write a statement which is too long for the spaces available on the form, most versions of FORTRAN allow you to continue it on the next line, starting at space 7. These are called **continuation lines,** and are usually indicated by a number in column 6. The number or symbol that you place in column 6 will vary with the version of FORTRAN that you are using. In the version used in this book the number 1 is placed in column 6 of the second line, the number 2 is placed in column 6 of the third line, and so on. Continuation lines may be used even if the statement does not need them. Take, for example, the statement:

```
      X=3.0*(A+B)+4.0*(C+D)+5.0*(E+F)
```

This statement could be spread over three lines, like this:

```
      X=3.0*(A+B)
     1+4.0*(C+D)
     2+5.0*(E+F)
```

8.4 Overflow

If a program attempts to print a number larger than has been allowed for in the **FORMAT** statement, we have **overflow.** For example, the largest integer that can be printed with **I5** in the **FORMAT** statement is + 9 999, and an attempt to print, say, 24 785 will lead to overflow. Most versions of FORTRAN will indicate overflow, although they will not all do it in the same way. In the example given, the computer used to run the programs in this book would output the symbol * instead of 24 785.

ASSIGNMENT 8.3

1. Write a program to read a row of six real numbers and to print them in a column.

2. Write a program to read a column of six real numbers and to print them in a row.

3. Write a program segment to read the nine numbers contained in the first three rows and the first three columns of a block of data containing more than three rows and columns of real numbers.

UNIT
9

Arrays

9.1 Input and Output of Arrays

There are many occasions in program writing when we need to deal with a large number of variables: we may need to work out the wages of several hundred people; or keep a record of the sale of different items in a large number of shops; or handle the results from an experiment. To enable the computer to deal with such programs, we use what are called **arrays.** Arrays are sometimes called **dimensioned variables.** In programming, the word *array* means a set of numbers.

Let us deal, for example, with twelve variables; we can call them, say, **A,B,C, ... ,** or we can use an array and call them **X(1), X(2)** and so on up to **X(12)**. The next program shows how the use of an array makes the **READ** and **WRITE** statements much shorter. Program 9.1 reads twelve numbers, calculates the sum of the 7th 8th and 9th numbers, prints the sum and then prints the twelve numbers.

The first line of the program, **DIMENSION X (12),** in effect says to the computer, "In this program we are going to use twelve numbers which we are calling **X(1), X(2), ... X(12)**." When the computer comes to the **READ** statement, it then knows that instead of only one value of **X** to read, there are twelve, and it reads the twelve numbers after ***DATA.** Remember that you must use a **FORMAT** statement which fits the way the data is arranged.

When the computer comes to the line **SUM** = **X(7)** + **X(8)** + **X(9),** it will take from its store the values of **X(7), X(8)** and **X(9),** add them together and assign to **SUM** the value 7.0 + 8.0 + 19.0 or 34.0. The line **WRITE (3,2) SUM** instructs the computer to print 34.0. The line **WRITE (3,3) X** instructs the computer to print the twelve values **X(1), X(2),** and so on. The **FORMAT** statement **3 FORMAT(1H ,4F10.4)** gives instructions to print out the twelve values of **X** in three lines with four values on each.

Since Program 9.1 contains an array of real numbers, the name of the array has to be of real type. We could have called it, say, **Y(12)** or

```
C       PROGRAM 9.1
        DIMENSION X(12)
        READ(2,1)X
      1 FORMAT(3F10.4)
        SUM=X(7)+X(8)+X(9)
        WRITE(3,2)SUM
        WRITE(3,3)X
      2 FORMAT(1H ,F10.4)
      3 FORMAT(1H ,4F10.4)
        END
*DATA
      1.0         2.0         3.0
      4.0         5.0         6.0
      7.0         8.0        19.0
      1.0         1.1         1.2
```

```
   34.0000
    1.0000    2.0000    3.0000    4.0000
    5.0000    6.0000    7.0000    8.0000
   19.0000    1.0000    1.1000    1.2000
```

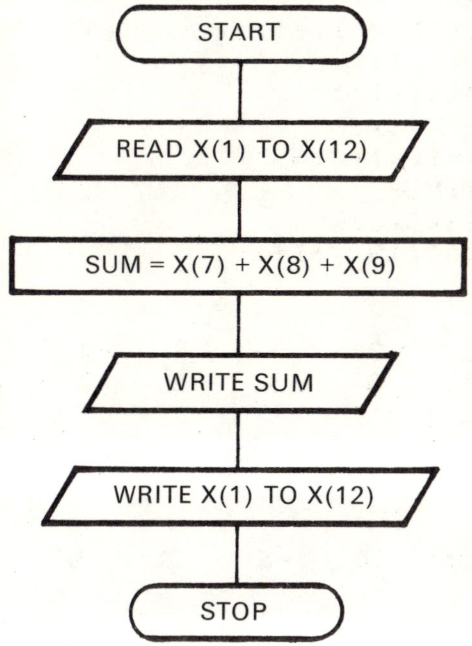

PRICE(12), but we could not have called it, for example, **N(12)** or **NUMBER(12)**. It is important to remember that the number indicating which member of the array we are dealing with (often called the subscript) must be in brackets: **X(6)** is correct, but **X6** is incorrect.

9.2 The use of DO Statements with Arrays

Program 9.2 shows the use of an array of integers. The program reads two arrays with six numbers in each; adds together the first number from each array, then the second number from each array, and so on; and finally prints these six sums.
The first line of the program tells the computer that the program will use the 18 integer variables **I(1)**, **I(2)**, ... , **I(6)**, **J(1)** to **J(6)** and **K(1)** to

```
C     PROGRAM 9.2
      DIMENSION I(6),J(6),K(6)
      READ(2,1)I,J
    1 FORMAT(6I5)
      DO 2 N=1,6
      K(N)=I(N)+J(N)
    2 CONTINUE
      WRITE(3,3)K
    3 FORMAT(1H.,6I5)
      END
*DATA
    2    5    7    3    8    9
    4    7    3   -5   -5    0
```

```
    6   12   10   -2    3    9
```

K(6). When the computer comes to **READ(2,1)I,J** it then knows that there are twelve values to be read in, (six values for **I** and six for **J**). At this stage of the program the six members of the array **K** have been assigned no values, because the computer has still to calculate those values.

The first time through the loop, **N** has the value 1, and the statement inside the loop becomes **K(1) = I(1) + J(1)**. Thus **K(1)** will be assigned the value 2 + 4 or 6. The second time through the loop, **K(2)** is assigned the value 12, the third time the value 10, and so on. The computer then comes to the **WRITE** statement and prints out the six values of **K**.

ASSIGNMENT 9.1

1. Write down the output of these program segments. The variables have the values assigned to them in Programs 9.1 and 9.2.

a.
```
      WRITE(3,4)X(1),X(2),X(3)
    4 FORMAT(1H ,3F5.1)
```

b.
```
      WRITE(3,4)I
    4 FORMAT(1H ,3I5)
```

2. What changes would be necessary in Program 9.2 to produce the output in column form?

3. Write down the output of these programs:

a.
```
      DIMENSION I(4),J(4)
      READ(2,1)I
    1 FORMAT(4I5)
      DO 2 N = 1,4
      J(N) = I(N)**2
      WRITE(3,3)J(N)
    3 FORMAT(1H ,I8)
    2 CONTINUE
      END
*DATA
   10   20   30   40
```

b.
```
      DIMENSION G(6)
      DO 1 N = 1,6
      READ(2,2)X
    2 FORMAT(F10.4)
      G(N) = X
    1 CONTINUE
      WRITE(3,3)G
    3 FORMAT(1H ,6F7.2)
      END
```

```
*DATA
  455.67
    -4.89
   46.4
     0.87
  -56.8
     4.11
```

c.
```
      DIMENSION I(5)
      DO 1 N = 1,5
      I(N) = 3*N
    1 CONTINUE
      WRITE(3,2)I
    2 FORMAT(1H  ,5I5)
      END
*DATA
```

9.3 The SUM of the Members of an Array

Program 9.3 reads an array of six numbers, calculates their sum and prints it out.

The first time through the loop, the value of **X(1)** is taken from store, and added to **SUM,** which has been given the initial value 0.0. **SUM** is then assigned the value 40.1. The second time through the loop, the value of **X(2)** is taken from store and added to **SUM,** which now takes the value 40.1 + 4.7, or 44.8. The third time through the loop, **SUM** takes the value 44.8 + 5.0 or 49.8. This continues until the sixth time through the loop, when **SUM** takes the value 62.5. The computer then leaves the loop and prints the value of **SUM.** (You may remember from Program 4.2 that both **FORMAT** statements can be kept to the end of the program, as in this example.)

```
C     PROGRAM 9.3
      DIMENSION X(6)
      READ(2,1)X
      SUM=0.0
      DO 2 N=1,6
      SUM=SUM+X(N)
    2 CONTINUE
      WRITE(3,3)SUM
    1 FORMAT(6F8.2)
    3 FORMAT(1H ,F10.2)
      END
*DATA
    40.1    4.7    5.0    4.9    5.2    2.6
```

```
      62.50
```

ASSIGNMENT 9.2

1. Explain what changes would be needed in Program 9.3 so that it would
(*a*) read the data in column form;
(*b*) read and add 500 numbers in column form;
(*c*) multiply instead of add the members of the array;
(*d*) find the sum of the squares of the array;
(*e*) read and add 400 numbers arranged in rows of 8 numbers.

ASSIGNMENT 9.3

1. Write a program to read an array with 100 real elements, multiply each member by 2.4, and print the new array.

2. Write a program to read three arrays, each with 50 real elements, add together the first members of each array, the second member of each array and so on, and to print the totals. (See Program 9.2.)

3. Write a program to read an array with twenty integer elements and calculate and print the average of its members.

***4.** Write a program to read an array of 200 integer members (in a single column) and to print the array in reverse order. (In a single column.)

***5.** Write a program to read, calculate and print the standard deviation of an array with 100 real elements.

Producing Titles and Headings

UNIT **10**

10.1 You will remember how to produce a heading on the listing of a program, using comment lines (see Unit 2). Many programs also require headings with the output, and these cannot be produced by comment lines alone. In this Unit you will learn how to produce headings in your output, paying special attention to the spacing of the results. To produce headings in output you will need to use a **Hollerith specification** in the **FORMAT** statement. The term *Hollerith* is used in recognition of the work of Dr. Herman Hollerith, who developed punched cards systems. (See the companion volume, *Primer of Computing*.)

Program 10.1 illustrates the use of a simple title:

```
C      PROGRAM 10.1
C      EXAMPLE OF HOLLERITH OUTPUT
       WRITE(3,1)
     1 FORMAT(1H ,41HTABLE OF SQUARES OF INTEGERS FROM 1 TO 10)
       END
*DATA
```

```
 TABLE OF SQUARES OF INTEGERS FROM 1 TO 10
```

When the computer comes to the **WRITE** statement, it notices that it is not followed by the names of any variables, and hence there are no numbers to print. When the computer comes to the **FORMAT** statement, the **41H** instructs it to output the 41 symbols immediately following the **H.** (You should notice that blank spaces are counted as symbols. If for example, **41H** was followed by 41 blank spaces, there would be 41 print positions left blank.)

If you need to place a heading on two lines, you can do so by using the slash which we studied in Unit 8. Program segment 10.2 illustrates this use of the slash:

```
C      PROGRAM 10.2
       WRITE(3,1)
     1 FORMAT(1H ,19HTABLE OF SQUARES OF/1H ,21HINTEGERS FROM 1 TO 10)
       END
*DATA
```

```
 TABLE OF SQUARES OF
 INTEGERS FROM 1 TO 10
```

Remember that the effect of a single slash in output **FORMAT** is to tell the computer that nothing else is to be printed out on that line.

The computer then looks for the next instruction, **1H ,** which instructs the printer to start the next section of output on a new line.‡

If you wish to have a blank line between two lines of a heading you may achieve this by replacing / by // in the **FORMAT** statement. If you need two blank lines, you replace / by ///, and so on.‡ Program segment 10.3 illustrates all these new procedures:

```
C      PROGRAM 10.3
       WRITE(3,1)
     1 FORMAT(1H ,41HTABLE OF SQUARES OF INTEGERS FROM 1 TO 10///1H ,16HI
      1NTEGER   SQUARE)
  ┌──→DO 2 N=1,10
  │    J=N**2
  │    WRITE(3,3)N,J
  │  3 FORMAT(1H ,I7,I9)
  └──2 CONTINUE
       END
*DATA
```

‡ The exact number of lines may vary with the computer system used. Consult the handbook for the computer in use

```
TABLE OF SQUARES OF INTEGERS FROM 1 TO 10


INTEGER   SQUARE
      1        1
      2        4
      3        9
      4       16
      5       25
      6       36
      7       49
      8       64
      9       81
     10      100
```

You will see that the **FORMAT** statement is too long to go on one line, and so it is continued on the next with a **continuation number** placed in column six (see Unit 8.3).

Since the headings **INTEGER** and **SQUARE** (together with the three spaces between them) require sixteen spaces, the field specifications in **3 FORMAT** have to be chosen carefully. For example, **3 FORMAT(1H ,2I8)** would have produced an untidy looking output, with the first column of figures under the space between **INTEGER** and **SQUARE.**

Before writing the **FORMAT** statements in your programs, you should plan the layout of the output on squared paper.

When you punch the Hollerith output, avoid making the least error, as it is difficult to delete. Indeed, some computers will not accept corrections in Hollerith output.

ASSIGNMENT 10.1

1. Rewrite **FORMAT (1H ,I7,I9)** in Program 10.3 to space the output as follows. (There are three spaces or print positions between **INTEGER** and **SQUARE.**)

```
INTEGER   SQUARE
      1        1
      2        4
. . . . . . . .
```

2. Write a program segment to produce the following heading:
CUBES AND SQUARES OF INTEGERS
INTEGER SQUARE CUBE

3. Write down the output of the following program segment.

```
  WRITE(3,5)
5 FORMAT(1H ,5HABCDE/1H ,5HFGHIJ//1H ,5HKLMNO///
  11H ,5HPQRST)
```

4. Find the errors in the following program segment, write a correct version, and write down the output.

```
  WRITE(2,3)
2 FORMAT(1H ,10HTABLES OF SQUARES,/11HAND CUBES)
```

10.2 Producing Blanks in Output

Sometimes we may wish to produce the following type of heading with, say, ten blank spaces between the three headings:

COST PRICE   SELLING PRICE   PROFIT

We can achieve this by using the following **FORMAT** statement:

```
FORMAT(1H ,49HCOST PRICE          SELLING PRICE          PROFIT)
```

To avoid this awkward layout, we can use instead the following **FORMAT** statement:

```
FORMAT(1H ,10HCOST PRICE,10X,13HSELLING PRICE,10X,6HPROFIT)
```

When the computer comes across **10X** in the **FORMAT** statement, it takes it as an instruction to leave the next ten spaces on that line blank. **6X** would be taken as an instruction to leave the next six spaces blank, and so on. Program segment 10.4 contains several examples of the use of the **X specification,** as it is called.

```
C     PROGRAM 10.4
C     AN EXAMPLE OF SPACING USING X SPECIFICATIONS
      WRITE(3,1)
    1 FORMAT(1H ,5HSMITH,5X,5HBROWN,5X,5HJONES//1H ,6HARCHER,4X,4HABEL,6
     1X,5HGREEN)
      END
*DATA
```

```
SMITH      BROWN      JONES

ARCHER     ABEL       GREEN
```

You should notice how important it is to use spaces carefully if you are to produce a properly spaced output.

ASSIGNMENT 10.2

1. Write down the **FORMAT** statement needed to produce the following output.

```
ONEbbbbbbTWObbbbbbTHREEbbbbFOUR
FIVE      SIX        SEVEN     EIGHT
NINE      TEN
```

The required blank spaces are indicated by b.

2. Write down the **FORMAT** statement needed to produce the following output.

```
ZZZZZ
 Z
  Z
   Z
```

3. Write down the output of the following program segment.

```
   WRITE(3,2)
 2 FORMAT(1H ,5X,36HSQUARE ROOTS OF NUMBERS FROM 1 TO 10
  1//1H ,10X,11HNUMBER ROOT)
```

ASSIGNMENT 10.3

***1.** Write a program to print a table of the squares, cubes, square roots and cube roots of the integers from 100 to 150. The output should be appropriately headed.

***2.** Write a program to print a table of the areas and circumferences of all circles with radii from 0.1 cm to 1.0 cm in steps of 0.1 cm. The output should be appropriately headed.

UNIT

11

Printing Headings and Numbers together

11.1 The last Unit showed how to produce Hollerith output. In this Unit you will learn how to produce Hollerith and numerical output on the same line. A simple program for doing this is shown in 11.1.

```
C       PROGRAM 11.1
C       OUTPUT OF HEADINGS AND NUMBERS TOGETHER
        N=7
        M=N**2
        J=N**3
        WRITE(3,1)N,M,J
      1 FORMAT(1H ,2HN=,I3,4X,10HN SQUARED=,I3,4X,8HN CUBED=,I4)
        END
*DATA
```

```
 N=   7    N SQUARED=  49    N CUBED=  343
```

The first three lines of the program assign the values 7,49 and 343 to **N**, **M** and **J** respectively; the **WRITE** statement tells the computer to print the values of **N**, **M** and **J**, and the **FORMAT** statement informs the computer how the Hollerith and numerical output has to be arranged. Let us see what each part of the **FORMAT** statement means:

1Hb Start a new line.
2H Print the two symbols following.
I3 Place the first value in the next three spaces.
4X Put in four spaces.
10H Print the ten symbols following.
I3 Place the second value in the next three spaces.

4X Put in four spaces.
8H Print the eight symbols following.
I4 Place the third value in the next four spaces.

You should notice that there is a comma after each part of the **FORMAT** statement and that, as usual, when an integer does not need all the spaces allocated, it is placed in the right of those spaces.
If we wish to have the output on three lines, we will have to rewrite the **FORMAT** statement like this:

FORMAT(1H ,2HN = ,I3/1H ,10HN SQUARED = ,I3/1H ,8HN CUBED = ,I4)

Once again, here is the meaning of each part of the **FORMAT** statement:

1Hb Start a new line.
2H Print the two symbols following.
I3 Place the first value in the next three spaces.
/ Terminate output on the first line.
1Hb Start a new line.
and so on.

Notice that when a slash is used, the comma is not needed at that point. This is how the output would appear:

N = 7
N SQUARED = 49
N CUBED = 343

ASSIGNMENT 11.1

1. Assuming that **PROFIT, COST, SALE** have the values 24.35, 49.62, 73.97, write a program segment to print:
PROFIT = 24.35 COST = 49.62 SALE = 73.97

2. With the values given in question 1, write a program segment to print out:
PROFIT = 24.35
COST = 49.62
SALE = 73.97

3. With the values given in question 1, write a program segment to print:
THE PROFITS AND COSTS ARE 24.35 AND 49.62 DOLLARS
SALE PRICE 73.97 DOLLARS

*11.2 An Example of Hollerith Output in Commercial Programming

The output of programs often has to be seen by many people. It is therefore important that the output be suitably headed, and well spaced. Program 11.2 works out the percentage increase or decrease in the sales of a product over the previous month's sales. (The program deals with the sales in only four towns, but it could readily be altered to cater for any number.) This is the kind of information that the managing director of a large firm might ask for during the first week of each month. Although the program looks a complicated way of producing the few lines of output required, you should remember that once the program has been written, only the two lines of data have to be input each time it is used.

```
C     PROGRAM 11.2
C     L=LAST MONTHS SALES.
C     LP=PREVIOUS MONTHS SALES.
C     P=PERCENTAGE INCREASE.
      DIMENSION L(4),LP(4),P(4)
      READ(2,1)L,LP
    1 FORMAT(4I5)
      DO 2 N=1,4
      X=L(N)
      Y=LP(N)
      P(N)=100.0*X/Y-100.0
    2 CONTINUE
      WRITE(3,3)LP,L,P
    3 FORMAT(1H ,44H        BATH    BRISTOL GLOUCESTER       LEEDS//1H ,4I
     111,2X,21HPREVIOUS MONTHS SALES/1H ,4I11,2X,17HLAST MONTHS SALES/1H
     2 ,4F11.2,2X,19HPERCENTAGE INCREASE)
      END
*DATA
 7000 5600 5700 2300
 7700 5200 5900 2350
```

```
        BATH    BRISTOL GLOUCESTER       LEEDS

        7700       5200       5900        2350  PREVIOUS MONTHS SALES
        7000       5600       5700        2300  LAST MONTHS SALES
       -9.09       7.69      -3.39       -2.13  PERCENTAGE INCREASE
```

The first operation that the computer will do is to read the four values **L(1) . . . . L(4)** and then the four values **LP(1) . . . . LP(4).** The **DO** loop is next used to calculate the four percentage increases. For example, the third time through the loop, **L(3)** and **LP(3)** have the values 5 700 and 5 900. Since these have to be changed to real form for the calculation, **X** and **Y** are assigned the values 5700.0 and 5900.0. The computer now calculates the percentage increase and we have

$$P(3) = \frac{100.0 \times 5700.0}{5900.0} - 100.0 = 96.61 - 100.0 = -3.39\%$$

You will see that a comment line has been used to explain the meaning of the three arrays. Each part of the **FORMAT** statement is explained below. (The numbers **1** and **2** in column six of the listing are continuation numbers —see Unit 8.3.)

1Hb	Start a new line.
44H	Print the 44 symbols following.
//	Terminate output on the first line and leave the next line blank.
1Hb	Start a new line.
4I11	Place the four values **LP(1)** to **LP(4)** in the next 44 spaces.
2X	Put in two spaces.
21H	Print the 21 symbols following.
/	Terminate output on that line.
1Hb	Start a new line.

and so on.

*ASSIGNMENT 11.2

1. Write a program segment to produce the following output, using the arrays and data in program 11.2:

```
 BATH   BRIS  GLOU  LEED
 7700   5200  5900  2350  PREVIOUS
 7000   5600  5700  2300  LAST
-9.09   7.69 -3.39 -2.13  INCREASE
```

2. Write a program to read the following ten integers and to print these integers together with their square roots correct to two decimal places, as shown:

```
INTEGERbbb567bbb345bbbb78bbb586bbb342bbbb46bbbbb4bbb456bbb362bbbb89
SQRTbbbb23.81b18.57 . . . . . . .
```

You will probably need to use an array and a **DO** loop.

The numbers should be input as a row.

3. Write a program to read the above integers arranged in a column and to print them together with their square roots as shown below. The program also has to produce the heading shown.

SQUARE ROOTS OF INTEGERS

INTEGERbbbSQUARE ROOT
bb567bbbbbbbb23.81
bb345bbbbbbbb18.57
bbb78bbbbbbbbb8.83
. . . .

*11.3 Spacing to the start of a new page

Most computers produce their printed output on listing paper which consists of a large number of separate pages joined by perforations, rather like a strip of giant postage stamps. It is sometimes necessary to produce the results of a program on several separate sheets. For example, you might wish to produce one page containing a table of squares, the next page a table of cubes, and so on. In order to make the printer start a new page, all you have to do is to replace **1Hb** by **1H1** at the correct point in the program. As soon as the computer comes to **FORMAT(1H1, ...)** the printer will go to the start of a new page even if it has printed only one or two lines on the current page.

More about FORTRAN Functions

UNIT **12**

12.1 In Unit 3 we studied one example of a FORTRAN function—the square root function, where the statement **Y** = **SQRT(X)** assigns the value of the square root of **X** to **Y**.

There are many other FORTRAN functions, but not all computers have the same functions **supplied** as part of the FORTRAN language. When you use a computer you will have to check that the functions that you intend to use are supplied. Some of the commoner supplied functions are dealt with in this Unit.

12.2 The SIN Function

If **X** is the size of an angle, the statement **Y** = **SIN(X)** will cause the computer to calculate the value of the sine of **X** and assign that value to **Y**. To use this function it is necessary to express the size of the angle in radians, not degrees. To do this you have to multiply the number of degrees by 0.017453 or $\pi/180$ (since $180° = \pi$ radians).

Program 12.1 shows how you can do the necessary arithmetic in the program itself. This program calculates the length of the side BC of the right-angled triangle ABC, given A = 60° and side AC = 3.64 cm.

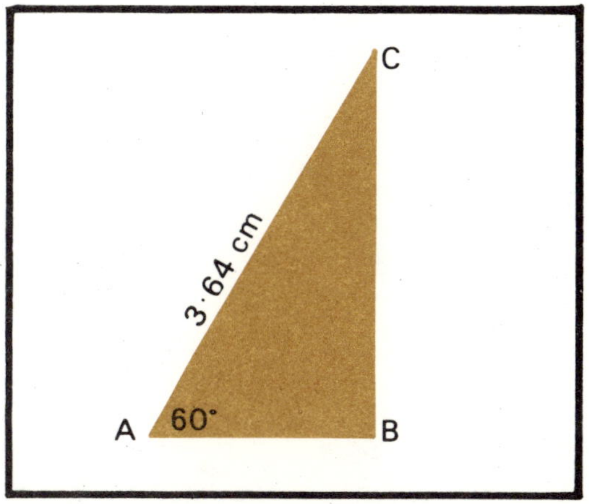

We use the fact that sin 60° = BC/AC, and that therefore BC = AC sin 60°.

```
C       PROGRAM 12.1
C       AN EXAMPLE OF THE SIN FUNCTION
        BC=3.64*SIN(0.017453*60.0)
        WRITE(3,2)BC
      2 FORMAT(1H ,F10.4)
        END
*DATA
```

```
      3.1523
```

Most computers will also supply a cosine function, usually written **COS(X)**. As before, the size of the angle must be expressed in radians. In both of these functions only real numbers can be used, and the values obtained are also real numbers.

ASSIGNMENT 12.1

1. Rewrite Program 12.1 so that the values of AC and angle A are read in as data.
2. Rewrite Program 12.1 to calculate the value of AB instead of BC.

12.3 Making Numbers Positive

In some programs it is necessary to make a negative number positive. If it is already positive it is left alone, but if it is negative, it is changed to become positive. This is done by using the **ABS** function. If, for example, **X** is equal to -8.5, then the statement **Y = ABS(X)** will assign to **Y** the value 8.5. If, however, **X** is equal to 57.0, then **Y** will be assigned the value 57.0.

If you are using integers, most computers will require the instruction **IABS** instead of **ABS**. For example, the statement **K = IABS(2**3 − 13)** would assign to **K** the absolute or positive value of $8-13$ which is of course $+5$. The use of the **ABS** function is illustrated in 12.4.

ASSIGNMENT 12.2

1. What value does the statement **Z = ABS(3.0*4.0 − 15.0)** assign to **Z**?
2. If **K** has the value 9, what value is assigned to **M** by the following statement? **M = IABS(6 − 3*K).**
3. What value is assigned to **Y** by the following statement?
   Y = ABS(78.0 − 68.0).
4. What value is assigned to **L** by the following statement? **L = ABS(−5).**

---

*12.4 Finding a Square Root by Successive Approximation

In many problems it may be difficult to find an exact answer, but easy to find an approximate answer. For example, if you are asked to find the square root of 17 without any tables or machines to help, you will probably take some time, although you can see that the answer will be just over 4.

In some types of problems, it is possible to use the approximate answer to find a more accurate answer, and then to use this new answer to find an even more accurate answer, and so on. This method could be used to find the square root of a number without using the **SQRT** function. (If you wish to know more about this method, you can find details in books on Numerical Methods.) It can be shown that if A is an approximation to the square root of X, a better approximation is given by the formula $A = \frac{1}{2}(A + X/A)$. Thus if we take 4 as an approximation to the square root of 17, a better approximation is given by $A = \frac{1}{2}(4 + 17/4)$ which has the value 4.125. This second approximation can be used again to give $A = \frac{1}{2}(4.125 + 17/4.125)$ which has the value 4.123. If this third approximation is used in the formula, the fourth approximation again comes to 4.123. So we have found that the square root of 17 is 4.123, correct to three decimal places. Program 12.2 finds the square root of 17 using this method. By changing the data we can use this program to find the square root of any number.

The purpose of the line **Y** = **A** is to store the previous value of **A** so that it can be compared with the new value. For example, when the loop is traversed for the second time, **Y** will be assigned the value 4.125 and **A** will be assigned the value 4.123. Since the answer to the question in the decision box is still **NO**, the loop will be traversed again.

You will see that the program prints each approximation. This is done so that the programmer can check that the solutions he gets are gradually approaching the final answer.

The purpose of the **IF** statement is to stop the program if the difference between two successive approximations is less than 0.0000001. The use of the **ABS** function is necessary since **(Y – A)** could produce a negative result, which would, of course, be less than 0.0000001. If, for example, **Y** has the value 4.2 and **A** the value 4.3, then **(Y – A)** will have the value – 0.1; as this value is less than 0.0000001, the program will stop, although the value of **A** which has been reached, 4.3, is not accurate enough. By using the **ABS** function, **(Y – A)** is assigned the positive value 0.1 which is not less than 0.0000001. Thus the possibility of receiving an incorrect result is avoided.

```
C       PROGRAM 12.2
        READ(2,1)X,A
      1 FORMAT(F10.4)
      2 Y=A
        A=(A+X/A)/2.0
        WRITE(3,3)A
      3 FORMAT(1H ,F10.6)
        IF(ABS(Y-A).LT.0.0000001)STOP
        GO TO 2
        END
*DATA
   17.0
    4.0
```

```
    4.125000
    4.123106
    4.123106
```

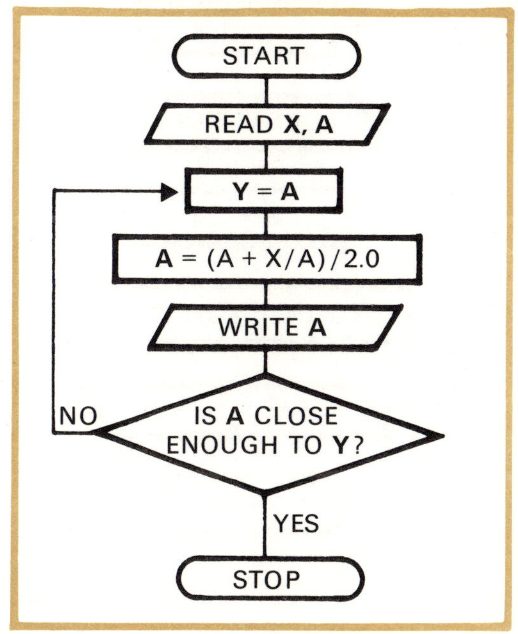

*ASSIGNMENT 12.3

1. Using arithmetic methods of successive approximation find the square root of 20 correct to two decimal places. Take 4 as the first approximation.
2. Rewrite Program 12.2 so that it will print the last approximation only.
3. If the version of FORTRAN that you are using does not have the **ABS** function, what alternative methods can you use to find the absolute value of a number?

ASSIGNMENT 12.4

1. Write a program to read a column of ten real numbers and to print those which are negative, but with the negative sign removed.
2. Rewrite Program 12.1 so that it will calculate the ten values of BC if the values of A go from 60° to 69° by steps of 1°.

*3. Write a program similar to 12.2, but with a **DO** loop instead of the **GO TO** statement. (The advantage of this method is that the program will stop after a stated number of approximations, and will not run on indefinitely if the **IF** statement is never satisfied. Hint: For the first run, limit your **DO** loop to 10 cycles.)

UNIT

13

More about DO Loops

13.1 So far our programs have required only one **DO** statement, but there are many problems which require several **DO** statements. The use of two **DO** statements is shown in Program 13.1, which reads a column of four figures and prints their squares.

The first **DO** loop reads the members of the array **X** one by one. For example, the third time through the loop the computer reads 1.3 and assigns this

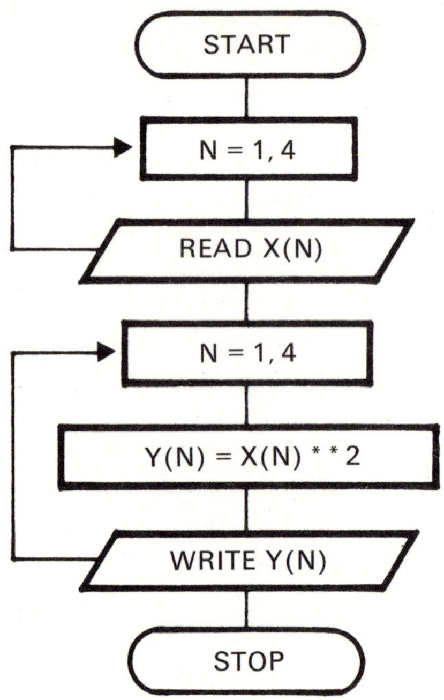


```
C       PROGRAM 13.1
        DIMENSION X(4),Y(4)
        DO 1 N=1,4
        READ(2,2)X(N)
      2 FORMAT(F5.1)
      1 CONTINUE
        DO 3 N=1,4
        Y(N)=X(N)**2
        WRITE(3,4)Y(N)
      4 FORMAT(1H ,F5.2)
      3 CONTINUE
        END
*DATA
    1.1
    1.2
    1.3
    1.4
```

```
    1.21
    1.44
    1.69
    1.96
```

value to **X(3)**. This is an alternative way of reading an array, as we could in fact replace the **DO** loop by

```
   READ(2,2)X
2  FORMAT(F5.1)
```

(See Unit 9)

The second loop in Program 13.1 calculates each square and then prints it before proceeding to the next number. For example, the second time through the loop, the computer takes the value of **X(2)** from its memory, squares it, assigns the value 1.44 to **Y(2)** and prints out this value.

ASSIGNMENT 13.1

1. Rewrite Program 13.1 so that it will deal with 400 numbers instead of 4.

2. Rewrite Program 13.1 so that it will print out the square roots instead of the squares.

13.2 Nested DO Loops

In Program 13.1 the two **DO** loops were separate from each other. It is also possible to have one **DO** loop inside another. These are called **nested DO** loops. In Program 13.2 nested loops are used to produce a multiplication table. The purpose of *CONTINUE* in the flow chart is to avoid having two lines coming from the *WRITE* box.

```
C     PROGRAM 13.2
      DO 1 N=30,32
      DO 2 M=30,32
      I=M*N
      WRITE(3,3)M,N,I
    3 FORMAT(1H ,I5,6H TIMES,I4,7H EQUALS,I5)
    2 CONTINUE
    1 CONTINUE
      END
*DATA
```

```
   30 TIMES  30 EQUALS  900
   31 TIMES  30 EQUALS  930
   32 TIMES  30 EQUALS  960
   30 TIMES  31 EQUALS  930
   31 TIMES  31 EQUALS  961
   32 TIMES  31 EQUALS  992
   30 TIMES  32 EQUALS  960
   31 TIMES  32 EQUALS  992
   32 TIMES  32 EQUALS 1024
```

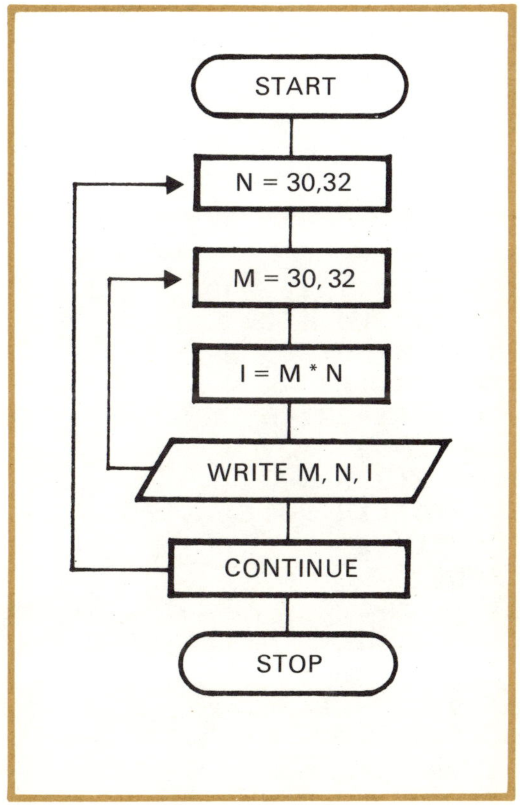

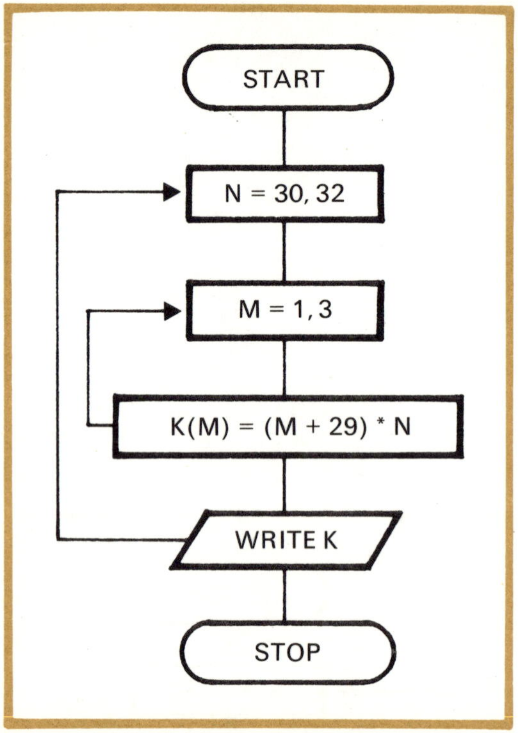


```
C       PROGRAM 13.3
        DIMENSION K(3)
        DO 1 N=30,32
        DO 2 M=1,3
        K(M)=(M+29)*N
      2 CONTINUE
        WRITE(3,3)K
      3 FORMAT(1H ,3I5)
      1 CONTINUE
        END
*DATA
```

```
   900  930  960
   930  961  992
   960  992 1024
```

At the start of this program, when the computer comes to the first **DO** loop, it will assign the value 30 to **N.** When the computer comes to the second **DO** loop, it will go through this loop three times, with **N** equal to 30, and with **M** equal to 30 the first time, 31 the second time, and 32 the third time. This means that **I** will be assigned the values 30 × 30, then 31 × 30, then 32 × 30.

When it has gone through the inner **DO** loop the required number of times, the computer will then go on to read the next line, **1 CONTINUE.** This is an instruction to go back to the beginning of the first **DO** loop and this time to give **N** the value 31. The next line, **DO 2 M = 30, 32,** introduces the second **DO** loop again, and the computer has to traverse this loop three times. This time, with the value 31 for **N, I** will now be assigned the values 30 × 31, 31 × 31, 32 × 31. When it has completed this cycle, the computer will again come to **1 CONTINUE,** and will return to the start of the first **DO** loop for the last time, giving **I** its last three remaining values, 30 × 32, 31 × 32, 32 × 32.

ASSIGNMENT 13.2

1. Rewrite Program 13.2 so that it will calculate the 36 products from 10 × 10 to 15 × 15.

2. Rewrite Program 13.2 so that it will calculate the 36 products from 1.0 × 1.0 to 1.5 × 1.5.

***3.** Rewrite Program 13.2 so that it will calculate the 12 products from 6.1 × 6.1 to 6.3 × 6.4.

We will now rewrite Program 13.2 to make it print the results on three lines instead of nine. To do this we need to have the complete line in store before we print it. This is done most conveniently by storing the line in an array, **K.**

We are using the value of **M** both in the calculation of the products and in the storage of the products in the array **K.** To do this, we give **M** the values 1, 2, 3, and obtain 30, 31, 32 by adding 29 in the assignment statement **K(M) = (M + 29)*N.**

N is first assigned the value 30 while the computer traverses the inner **DO** loop three times, carrying out the following three calculations:
K(1) = (1 + 29)*30 = 900
K(2) = (2 + 29)*30 = 930
K(3) = (3 + 29)*30 = 960

The computer now leaves the inner **DO** loop and comes to the instruction **WRITE(3,3)K,** which produces the first line of output. **N** is now assigned the value 31, and the three new values of the array **K** are calculated and printed in the second line of the output. Finally, with the value 32 for **N**, the third line is calculated and printed.

ASSIGNMENT 13.3

1. Rewrite Program 13.3 so that it will print, in a table of 6 rows and 6 columns, the 36 products from 10 × 10 to 15 × 15.
2. Rewrite Program 13.3 so that it will print the output in a single column.

13.3 Providing Headings

The results of Program 13.3 are printed without any headings. One part of the headings for a table is a statement of the values involved in each row and column. This is illustrated in Program 13.4. This program calculates the longest side (the hypotenuse) of all the right-angled triangles with integer sides up to and including 5. We use the rule of Pythagoras, which states that the square on the hypotenuse is equal to the sum of the squares on the other two sides. If, for example, the two shortest sides are 3 and 4, the length of the hypotenuse (H), can be found from the formula
$H = \sqrt{(3^2 + 4^2)} = 5$.

```
C     PROGRAM 13.4
      DIMENSION H(5)
      WRITE(3,4)
    4 FORMAT(1H ,5X,1H1,6X,1H2,6X,1H3,6X,1H4,6X,1H5)
      DO 1 N=1,5
      DO 2 M=1,5
      X=N
      Y=M
      H(M)=SQRT(X**2+Y**2)
    2 CONTINUE
      WRITE(3,3)N,H
    3 FORMAT(1H ,I2,5F7.3)
    1 CONTINUE
      END
*DATA
```

```
       1      2      3      4      5
 1 1.414  2.236  3.162  4.123  5.099
 2 2.236  2.828  3.606  4.472  5.385
 3 3.162  3.606  4.243  5.000  5.831
 4 4.123  4.472  5.000  5.657  6.403
 5 5.099  5.385  5.831  6.403  7.071
```

The computer first prints out the heading using the first **FORMAT** statement. The purpose of each part of the statement is as follows:

1Hb	Space to the start of a new line
5X	Leave the next 5 print positions blank
1H1	Print "1" in the next space
6X	Leave the next six print positions blank

and so on.

The computer then enters the first **DO** loop, giving **N** the value 1. The computer proceeds to traverse the inner **DO** loop, to produce the first five members of the array like this:

H(1) = **SQRT** $(1.0^2 + 1.0^2) = 1.414$
H(2) = **SQRT** $(1.0^2 + 2.0^2) = 2.236$
H(3) = **SQRT** $(1.0^2 + 3.0^2) = 3.162$

and so on for **H(4)** and **H(5)**.

The computer now prints the array with the value of **N** at the beginning of the line.

The computer goes on to assign the value 2 to **N** and again traverses the inner **DO** loop five times to produce five new values for **H(1)** to **H(5)**. It prints these as the next line of the output. The last three lines are produced in the same way, with **N** = 3, 4, 5. The two lines, **X** = **N** and **Y** = **M**, are necessary as most compilers will not accept integers in a **SQRT** function.

ASSIGNMENT 13.4

1. What changes would be necessary in Program 13.4 so that it would print the results for triangles with sides of length from 0.1 to 1.0, increasing by steps of 0.1?

2. Write down the output of this program:

```
      DO 1 I = 1,3
      DO 2 N = 1,I
      WRITE(3,3)N
    3 FORMAT(1H ,I2)
    2 CONTINUE
    1 CONTINUE
      END
*DATA
```

3. Rewrite Program 13.3 so that it has the columns and the rows headed by the numbers 30 to 32.

3.4 Correct and incorrect use of Multiple DO Loops

There are certain rules to be followed when **DO** loops are placed inside one another. If the arrows drawn from the **CONTINUE** to the **DO** do not cross, the **DO** loops are being used in a permissible manner; but if these lines do cross, the loops are being used wrongly and the program will not work.

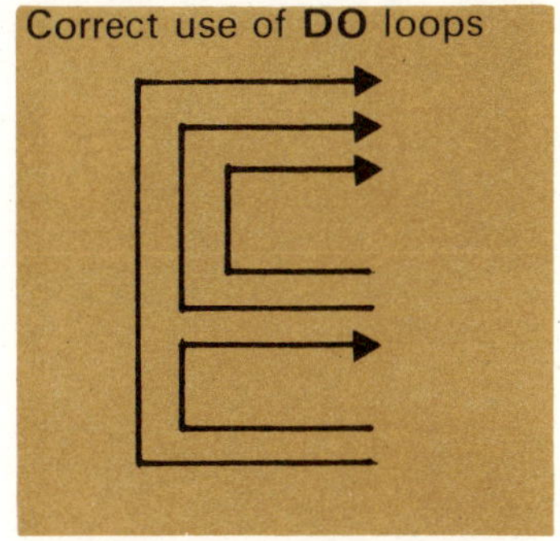

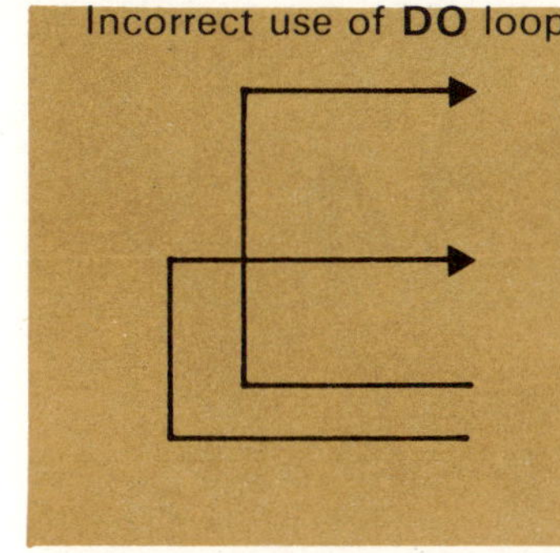

Sometimes it is necessary to jump out of a **DO** loop, using a **GO TO** statement. Again there are rules that must be followed. You may jump out of a **DO** loop, or you may jump from one point to another in the same loop, but you may not jump into a loop from outside.

If you write a program which contains a lot of **DO** loops and jumps, you should consult a book on advanced FORTRAN programming, which will deal with **DO** loops in more detail. (See the book mentioned in 15.3.)

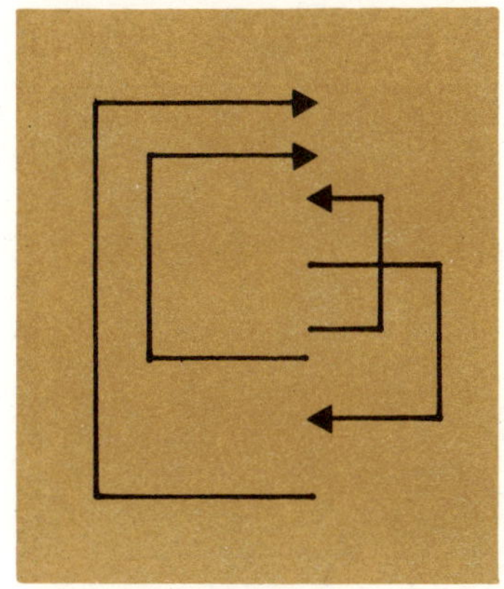

CORRECT

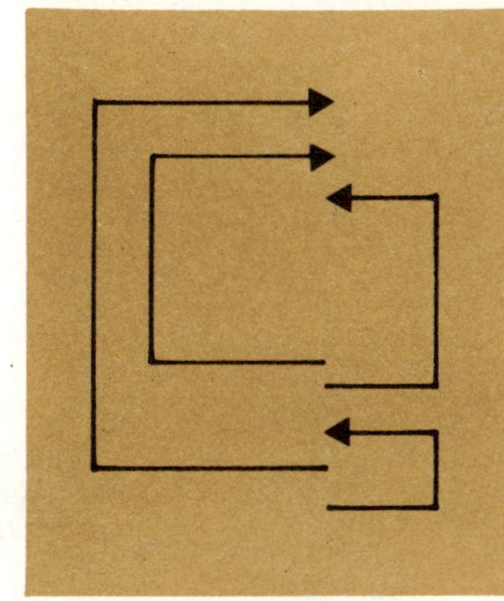

INCORRECT

*ASSIGNMENT 13.5

Write a program to print a table of the masses of cones with base radii 1(1)10cm (This means from 1cm to 10cm in steps of 1cm), heights 2(2)10cm, and density 1.0(0.1)2.0gm/cm². The table should be printed out on eleven separate pages, one for each density, and the table should have 5 columns, one for each height. The whole table, and the columns on each page, should be provided with suitable headings. Use should be made of mixed Hollerith and numerical output to produce such headings as: **DENSITY = 1.1 GM.PER SQR CM.**

.F.B.—F

UNIT
14

More about Arrays

14.1 In Unit 9 we discussed arrays. We saw how to use these arrays when we wished to avoid having to list a large number of variables in a long **READ** statement. The arrays that we have used so far are called **one-dimensional** arrays. In this Unit you will learn how to use **two-dimensional** arrays. Two dimensions are involved, for example, in a table giving a column of pupils' names (one variable), with a row of examination marks (the second variable) beside each name; or in a table showing petrol costs, where the number of litres bought (one variable) is listed down the side, and the price per litre (the second variable) is shown along the top of the table. (You can see a table of this type in 14.4 on page 86.)

```
C       PROGRAM 14.1
        DIMENSION I(3,2)
        READ(2,1) I
      1 FORMAT(3I5)
        WRITE(3,2)I
      2 FORMAT(1H ,3I4)
        WRITE(3,3)I(2,1),I(3,2)
      3 FORMAT(1H ,2I5)
        END
*DATA
   23   45   13
   17    9  -17
```

```
  23  45  13
  17   9 -17
   45  -17
```

Program 14.1 illustrates how to read and print a two-dimensional array, and also how to print given members of the array.

The statement **DIMENSION I (3,2)** informs the computer that it must regard **I**, not as a single number, but as a set of six numbers arranged in three columns and two rows like this:

	Col. 1	Col. 2	Col. 3
Row 1	I(1,1)	I(2,1)	I(3,1)
Row 2	I(1,2)	I(2,2)	I(3,2)

When the computer comes to the **READ** statement, it reads the six values for **I** in the required order, giving **I(1,1)** the value 23, **I(2,1)** the value 45, and so on. **FORMAT** statement **1** informs the computer that numbers are provided in rows containing three integers, with five spaces allocated to each.

When the computer comes to the first **WRITE** statement, it again knows that it has to print not one value for **I**, but all six values. **FORMAT** statement **2** tells the computer to do this in rows of three integers with four spaces allocated to each.

The second **WRITE** statement instructs the computer to print two members of the array. **I(2,1)** is the number from the second column and the first row, and **I(3,2)** is the number from the third column and second row. **FORMAT** statement **3** tells the computer to print these numbers in a row of two integers with five spaces allocated to each.

If we wish to print the whole of, say, the first row, we must include the following statements:

```
   WRITE(3,4),I(1,1),I(2,1),I(3,1)
4  FORMAT(1H ,3I5)
```

(See the note at the side of the page.)

ASSIGNMENT 14.1

1. Write a program to read the following array and then to print the first number in the first row, the second number in the second row, and the third number in the third row. These three numbers are to be printed on one line.

   12bbb14bb167
   45bb345bbb67
   64bbb34bbb27

2. Write a program to read the following array and to print the middle row as a row, and the last column as a column.

5.6	3.3	2.7	2.8
0.8	–2.5	5.7	3.2
2.9	1.0	0.6	–3.9

4.2 To Print a row or a column from an Array

The methods just shown will produce rather long programs if the arrays involved are large. The length of the program can be reduced, however, by using **DO** statements. Program 14.2 uses a **DO** statement to read an array and print the fourth column.

After the computer has read the fifteen members of the array, it then comes to the **DO** loop. The first time through the loop, **N** takes the value 1, and the computer will print **M(4,1)**, that is the number 32. The second time through the loop, it will print **M(4,2)** and so on. Each of these three numbers will be printed on a new line as instructed in the **FORMAT** statement.

If we wish to print the third row, here is the relevant section of the program:

```
   DO 2 N = 1,5
   WRITE(3,3) M(N,3)
3  FORMAT(1H ,I5)
```

NOTE
In this book the first subscript in a two-dimensional array refers to the column, and the second subscript to the row. This has the advantage that the array can easily be read in the correct way up, that is row by row.

In many other books the first subscript refers to the row and the second subscript to the column. This has the disadvantage that the array has to be input in column order, that is the array has to be transposed. It is possible to input it the "correct" way up, but the **READ** statement is then more complicated.

If this second method is used with Program 14.1, then:
DIMENSION I(3,2) and **WRITE(3,3) I(2,1),I(3,2)** will have to be changed to
DIMENSION I(2,3) and **WRITE(3,3) I(1,2),I(2,3)** and the array will have to be arranged for input in column order—that is, the numbers in column one, followed by the numbers in column two, and the numbers in column three, as follows:

```
23   17
45    9
13  - 17
```

It will also appear this way up on output.

```
C      PROGRAM 14.2
C      TO OUTPUT A COLUMN FROM AN ARRAY
       DIMENSION M(5,3)
       READ(2,1)M
     1 FORMAT(5I5)
       DO 2 N=1,3
       WRITE(3,3)M(4,N)
     3 FORMAT(1H ,I5)
     2 CONTINUE
       END
*DATA
   23   45   67   32   15
    3    5   23  256  -34
   56  347 -567   46    0
```

```
   32
  256
   46
```

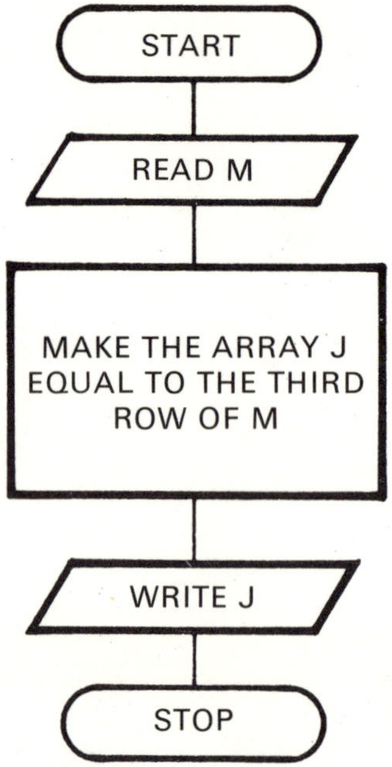

As instructed in the **FORMAT** statement, the values of **M(1,3), M(2,3), M(3,3), M(4,3), M(5,3)** will be printed in column form. If we wish to print all the numbers in one row, we can do this by storing them in a separate one-dimensional array, and then printing the new array on a single line. Program 14.3 reads an array and then prints the third row.

```
C      PROGRAM 14.3
C      TO OUTPUT A ROW FROM AN ARRAY
       DIMENSION M(5,3),J(5)
       READ(2,1)M
     1 FORMAT(5I5)
       DO 2 N=1,5
       J(N)=M(N,3)
     2 CONTINUE
       WRITE(3,3)J
     3 FORMAT(1H ,5I5)
       END
*DATA
   23   45   67   32   15
    3    5   23  256  -34
   56  347 -567   46    0
```

```
   56  347 -567   46    0
```

The first time through the loop, the computer, following the instruction **J(1)** = **M(1,3)**, takes from its store the value of **M(1,3)** and assigns this value to **J(1)**. This gives **J(1)** the value 56. The second time through the loop, **J(2)** is assigned the value 347 and so on.

The **WRITE** statement instructs the computer to print the five values **J(1)** to **J(5)**, and the **5I5** in the **FORMAT** statement ensures that the output is on one line.

ASSIGNMENT 14.2

1. What alteration would be required in Program 14.3 to print out the second row instead of the third?
2. Rewrite Program 14.3 so that it prints out the second and third rows with the third row directly under the second.

3. Rewrite Program 14.3 so that it prints out the second and third rows with the second row directly under the third.

4. Rewrite Program 14.2 so that it prints out the second and fourth columns. The fourth column should be placed immediately to the right of the second column.

14.3 The Sum of a row or column from an Array

A 4 by 3 array is shown in the data for Program 14.4 (i.e. an array with 4 columns and 3 rows). This array will be stored in array **L.** If we wish to find the sum of the second column, we need to add together the following members of the array **L(2,1), L(2,2), L(2,3).** This is best done using a **DO** statement, a method that can be applied to arrays of any size.

The sum of the second column of data is to be assigned to **N**, and before using **N** in the **DO** loop, we must give it the value 0.

The first time through the loop, the value of **L(2,1)** is taken from store and added to **N.** This gives **N** the value 0 + 53, that is 53. The second time through the loop, the value of **L(2,2)** is added to **N.** This gives **N** the value 23 + 53 or 76. The last time through the loop, the value of **L(2,3)** is added to **N**, giving **N** the value 76 + 13 or 89. You will see that a slight alteration to the **DO** statement will enable this program to deal with an array of any size.

```
C       PROGRAM 14.4
C       THE SUM OF ONE COLUMN OF AN ARRAY
        DIMENSION L(4,3)
        READ(2,1) L
      1 FORMAT(4I5)
        N=0
        DO 2 I=1,3
        N=N+L(2,I)
      2 CONTINUE
        WRITE(3,3)N
      3 FORMAT(1H ,I10)
        END
*DATA
   12     53     28     9
    5     23     19     5
    2     13      9     2
```

```
        89
```

ASSIGNMENT 14.3

1. Rewrite the Program 14.4 so that it will total the fourth column instead of the second.

2. Rewrite Program 14.4 so that it will total the third row.

3. Rewrite Program 14.4 so that it will total the seventh row of an array with 10 columns and 10 rows.

4. Write a program that will read an array with 10 columns and 20 rows, calculate the square of each member of the array, and print the results in similar array form.

---

*14.4 The use of an Array in a Data Processing problem

Arrays are useful in programs designed to handle tables, for example, to calculate the value of the stocks held by a factory or a chain of shops. Program 14.5 shows a simplified calculation of this type; although it deals with only three shops and four items, this program could readily be altered to deal with dozens of shops, each stocking hundreds of items. Once the program has been written, it can be used repeatedly with different data. From the total number of items in each shop, the computer will be able to calculate the value of the stock in each shop in a few seconds. This table shows the data that the computer processes.

	Tables	*Chairs*	*Cupboards*	*Beds*
Shop A	12	53	28	9
Shop B	5	23	19	5
Shop C	2	13	9	2
Price in new pence	2300	850	2000	1025

We will now consider in detail the problem of calculating the value of the goods held by each shop. The details of the stock held by the shops will be read to a 4 by 3 array called **NUMBER**; and the prices of each of the four stock items will be read to an array called **IPRICE**.

To find the value of the items in the first shop, we have to calculate **NUMBER(1,1)*IPRICE(1)** + **NUMBER(2,1)*IPRICE(2)** + **NUMBER (3,1)*IPRICE(3)** + **NUMBER(4,1)*IPRICE(4)**. Similar expressions will enable us to find the value of the items in the other two shops. For repetitive calculations like these, we can use two **DO** statements. The first or outer **DO** loop specifies the shop (the second time through the loop, for example, the value of the goods in the second shop is calculated). The second, or inner **DO** loop, calculates the values of each item for the given shop, and totals these values.

There are several points to notice here. We have used more than one letter for the name of the array. This is common practice in long programs in order to help the programmer to remember what each array stands for. We have used the letter I as the first character of the first two names so that they may represent integer numbers. (At the end of this Unit we will see another way of dealing with this.) The prices have been given in new pence, so that they can be written as integers. In this way we avoid a mixture of real and integer numbers in the arithmetic.

Let us consider what happens when the outer **DO** loop is traversed for, say, the second time. Initially **IVALUE(2)** (which will be the value of the goods sold by the second shop) is given the value 0. The first time through the inner loop, it is assigned the value 0 + **NUMBER(1,2)*IPRICE(1)**, or

```
C       PROGRAM 14.5
        DIMENSION NUMBER(4,3),IPRICE(4),IVALUE(3),RVALUE(3)
        READ(2,3)NUMBER,IPRICE
      3 FORMAT(4I10)
        DO 1 N=1,3
        IVALUE(N)=0
        DO 2 M=1,4
        IVALUE(N)=IVALUE(N)+NUMBER(M,N)*IPRICE(M)
      2 CONTINUE
        RVALUE(N)=IVALUE(N)
        RVALUE(N)=RVALUE(N)/100.0
      1 CONTINUE
        WRITE(3,4)RVALUE
      4 FORMAT(1H ,3F10.2)
        END
*DATA
        12        53        28         9
         5        23        19         5
         2        13         9         2
      2300       850      2000      1025
```

```
   1378.75    741.75    357.00
```

5 × 2300; the second time through the inner loop, it is assigned the value 5 × 2300 + **NUMBER(2,2)*IPRICE(2)**, or 5 × 2300 + 23 × 850; the third time, it is assigned the value 5 × 2300 + 23 × 850 + **NUMBER(3,2)*IPRICE(3)**, or 5 × 2300 + 23 × 850 + 19 × 2000; and the last time, it is assigned the value 5 × 2300 + 23 × 850 + 19 × 2000 + **NUMBER(4,2)*IPRICE(4)**, or 5 × 2300 + 23 × 850 + 19 × 2000 + 5 × 1025.

The statements after **2 CONTINUE** change **IVALUE(2)** to a real number so that it can be divided by 100.0 to change to £.

14.5 To Read a large Array

As the FORTRAN coding form has only a limited number of columns, there could be some difficulty in reading arrays with a large number of columns. To show how we may tackle this problem, let us take the following array:

```
3 5 6 3 7 6
3 6 9 6 2 7
4 2 6 8 4 9
```

We could read in this by starting our program:

```
   DIMENSION I(6,3)
   READ(2,1)I
1  FORMAT(6I2)
```

but we could also read it in this way:

```
3 5 6
3 7 6
3 6 9
6 2 7
4 2 6
8 4 9
```

with the program starting:

```
   DIMENSION I(6,3)
   READ(2,1)I
1  FORMAT(3I2)
```

In both cases the computer knows that it has to read the 18 members of the array **I**. It does not matter which way the array is arranged provided that the correct **FORMAT** statement is used, and that the numbers are in the correct order. You should remember that the computer will read in the first row of data, and then the second, and so on. Since the program starts with **DIMENSION I(6,3)** it will still treat the array as having six columns and three rows.

*ASSIGNMENT 14.4

1. A program has to read an array **J(100,50)**. Each member of the array is to be read with **I5 FORMAT.** Write a program segment to read this

array so as to occupy as few lines as possible. (Remember that the coding form is only 72 spaces across.)

2. Rewrite Program 14.5 so that it will also calculate the total value of the goods sold by all the shops. Use a **DO** loop.

14.6 Type Statements

You will remember that particular letters or combinations of letters have to be used for integer or real numbers. For example, earlier in this Unit we had to use **IVALUE** to represent an integer number; this was rather inconvenient, and it would have been neater if we could have used **VALUE.** This difficulty can be overcome by using a **type statement.** In the case mentioned above, if the program using **VALUE** is written, the statement **INTEGER VALUE** must appear before **VALUE** is used for the first time. After this type statement, the computer will treat **VALUE** as integer. A **REAL** type statement is demonstrated in Program 14.6.

```
C       PROGRAM 14.6
C       AN EXAMPLE OF A TYPE STATEMENT
        REAL I
        READ(2,1)I,R
      1 FORMAT(2F5.1)
        E=I*R
        WRITE(3,2)E
      2 FORMAT(1H ,F10.4)
        END
*DATA
  4.2   3.5
```

```
      14.7000
```

Because the program starts with **REAL I,** you will see that **I** can then be treated as **REAL**; for example, it is assigned the **REAL** value 4.2. It is possible to start a program with more than one type statement; for example, in a program which starts with:

INTEGER A,B,X
REAL J,K

The values of **A,B,X** are regarded as **INTEGER** and **J,K** as **REAL** numbers.

ASSIGNMENT 14.5

What type statements are needed at the start of this program if it is to be used with the given data?

```
      READ(2,1)X,Y,I,J,K
    1 FORMAT(2I5,3F5.1)
      Z = X*Y
      A = I*J*K
      WRITE(3,2)Z,A
    2 FORMAT(1H ,I10,F10.4)
      END
*DATA
   34   45   5.6   7.3   4.9
```

*Handling Characters and Drawing Graphs

*UNIT 15

15.1 So far in producing headings or names in our programs, we have used Hollerith output. There are certain types of problem, however, in which the use of Hollerith output would make the program very complicated. If we were listing examination results, for example, we might want the computer to print both the names and the marks of the candidates in the order of their position in the examination.

For this type of program we need to be able to read and print names in the same way as we read and print numbers. We can do this using **alphanumeric character** input and output.

Program 15.1 shows simply how to use alphanumeric characters. The program reads two names and prints them in reverse order. You will see that the **FORMAT** statements contain **A** in place of **F**, **I**, or **H**. This is because we are dealing with characters and not with numbers. In computing language we are dealing with **character fields**, not **number fields**.

FORMAT(2A5) is an instruction to the computer to take the first five characters of data, in this case **SMITH**, and assign this "value" to **NAME1**; then to take the next five characters, in this case **BROWN**, and assign this "value" to **NAME2**. These "values" cannot, of course, be used for calculation. All that the computer can do with them is to print them out again, and this is done with the order reversed.

Program 15.2 is an alternative version of Program 15.1. The only difference is in the **FORMAT** statements: the **2A5** in Program 15.1 requires the variables to be given two per line (or per card), whereas the **A5** in Program 15.2 requires them to be one value per line. (This is similar to using, say **2I5** and **I5** with integers.)

There are two important points that you must remember. Firstly, the maximum number of characters permitted in an alphanumeric variable depends on the model of computer being used. In this Unit we will assume the maximum number is six. Secondly, with some computers (including the one used to test the programs in this book), the alphanumeric variables

```
C     PROGRAM 15.1
      READ(2,1)NAME1,NAME2
    1 FORMAT(2A5)
      WRITE(3,2)NAME2,NAME1
    2 FORMAT(1H ,2A5)
      END
*DATA
SMITHBROWN
```

```
 BROWNSMITH
```

```
C     PROGRAM 15.2
      READ(2,1)I,J
    1 FORMAT(A5)
      WRITE(3,2)J,I
    2 FORMAT(1H ,A5)
      END
*DATA
SMITH
BROWN
```

```
 BROWN
 SMITH
```

must be integer variables and begin with **I, J, K, L, M** or **N**. If we wished to call the variables in the last two programs **WORD1** and **WORD2**, we would have to start the program with the type statement **INTEGER WORD1,WORD2** (see Unit 14).

As you will see in Assignment 15.1, no. 2, the characters used in data for the alphanumeric variables are not restricted to those of the alphabet, and we may use any symbol (such as * or /) that the computer prints.

ASSIGNMENT 15.1

1. Write down the output of the following program.

```
     READ(2,1)I,J,K,L
   1 FORMAT(2A6)
     WRITE(3,2)I,J,K,L
   2 FORMAT(1H ,4A6)

*DATA
FRED   OXO
TED    BRANDY
```

2. Write down the output of the following program.

```
     INTEGER DOT,CROSS,SPACE,STAR
     READ(2,1)DOT,CROSS,SPACE,STAR
   1 FORMAT(4A1)
     WRITE(3,2)DOT,DOT,DOT,CROSS,CROSS,CROSS,STAR,SPACE,STAR
   2 FORMAT(1H ,3A1)

*DATA
.X *
```

(In this program we use the variable name **STAR** to refer to the symbol *; but any name which suits our convenience could be used; we could, for example, have used **SHAPE4.** Similarly for the other two symbols and the blank space.)

15.2 A Data Processing Example

Let us apply what we have learned so far in this Unit to a banking situation. We are going to write a program to read a list of names together with the corresponding bank balances, and print out a list of those with overdrafts, i.e. negative balances.

Program 15.3 uses a **DO** statement to read a set of names and balances. As each balance is read, it is examined to see if it is negative, in which case it is printed together with its associated name.

```
C      PROGRAM 15.3
       DO 1 N=1,5
       READ(2,2)NAME,BAL
     2 FORMAT(A6,F10.2)
       IF(BAL.GE.0.0)GO TO 1
       WRITE(3,4)NAME,BAL
     4 FORMAT(1H ,A6,F10.2)
     1 CONTINUE
       END
*DATA
BROWN       45.36
SMITH      -34.00
HOSKIN      45.35
GREEN       -4.37
ARCHER       5.49
```

```
 SMITH      -34.00
 GREEN       -4.37
```

With this program a difficulty arises because each name is restricted to the maximum of six characters. This means that names like Williams would have to be abbreviated. This difficulty can be overcome, however, in the way shown in program 15.4, which reads and prints a line of words or symbols.

```
C       PROGRAM 15.4
        DIMENSION N(12)
        READ(2,1)N
      1 FORMAT(12A6)
        WRITE(3,2)N
      2 FORMAT(1H ,6A6)
        END
*DATA
THIS PROGRAM IS AN EXAMPLE OF THE INPUT AND OUTPUT OF A LINE OF TEXT.
```

```
THIS PROGRAM IS AN EXAMPLE OF THE IN
PUT AND OUTPUT OF A LINE OF TEXT.
```

The line of words is regarded as an array of alphanumeric variables, each one occupying six spaces.

The **READ** statement instructs the computer to read the twelve elements of the array **N**. The first element, **N(1)**, contains the symbols **THIS P** (notice that the space is counted as one of the six characters); the second element, **N(2)**, contains **ROGRAM**; and so on. If the line of input is less than 72 characters long, the last elements of the array will consist of blanks. You will see that the second **FORMAT** statement contains **6A6** instead of **12A6**. This causes the output to be placed on two lines instead of one.

ASSIGNMENT 15.2

1. Write a program to read a row of names and print them as a column. Each name can have up to six letters and there are ten names on the line.
2. Write a program to read a row of ten letters or symbols and to print them in a row, but in reverse order.
3. Write a program which will read a 10 by 10 array of symbols (i.e. 100 symbols in all) and print them with rows and columns transposed (i.e. a symbol in the sixth row and ninth column will be moved to the ninth row and sixth column).

15.3 Drawing Graphs using a Computer

Sometimes it is necessary to produce a graph using a computer. The best way of doing this is by using a **digital plotter,** which draws the graphs by moving a pen over paper under the control of the computer. The graphs drawn by digital plotters are very accurate, but as a digital plotter can cost several thousand pounds, many computer installations do not have one. Most computers, however, can produce graphs consisting of dots or crosses.

Program 15.5 plots the graph of $y = x(16 - x)$ from $x = 0$ to $x = 16$ with the Y-axis across the page and X-axis down the page. The program works on the following basis: the first value of x is taken, in this case 0, and the value of y is calculated, which also comes to 0. The computer then places a symbol, such as a star or a dot, in position zero. The second value of x is taken and y is assigned the value $1(16 - 1)$ which comes to 15. The computer then places the symbol in position fifteen. This procedure is repeated for the other values of x.

This method of drawing graphs has the disadvantage that only integer points can be plotted; for example, the symbol may not be placed in

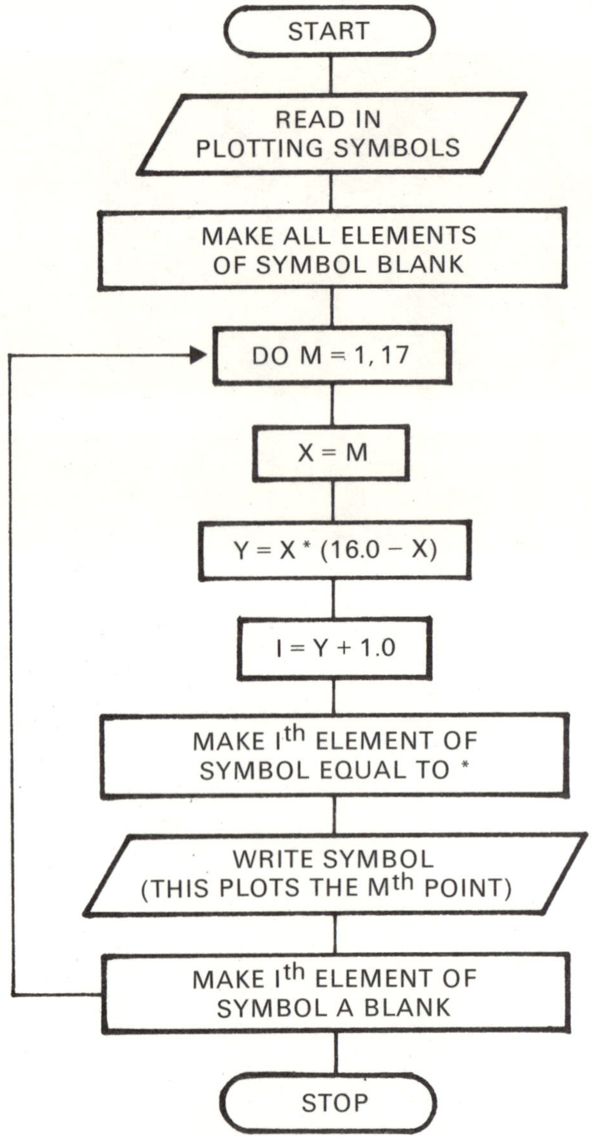


```
C         PROGRAM 15.5
C         GRAPH OF Y=X*(16.0-X)
          INTEGER BLANK,DOT,SYMBOL
          DIMENSION SYMBOL(65)
          READ(2,1)BLANK,DOT
        1 FORMAT(2A1)
          DO 2 N=1,65
          SYMBOL(N)=BLANK
        2 CONTINUE
          DO 3 M=1,17
          X=M-1
          Y=X*(16.0-X)
          I=Y+1.0
          SYMBOL(I)=DOT
          WRITE(3,4)SYMBOL

        4 FORMAT(1H ,65A1)
          SYMBOL(I)=BLANK
        3 CONTINUE
          END
*DATA
 *
```

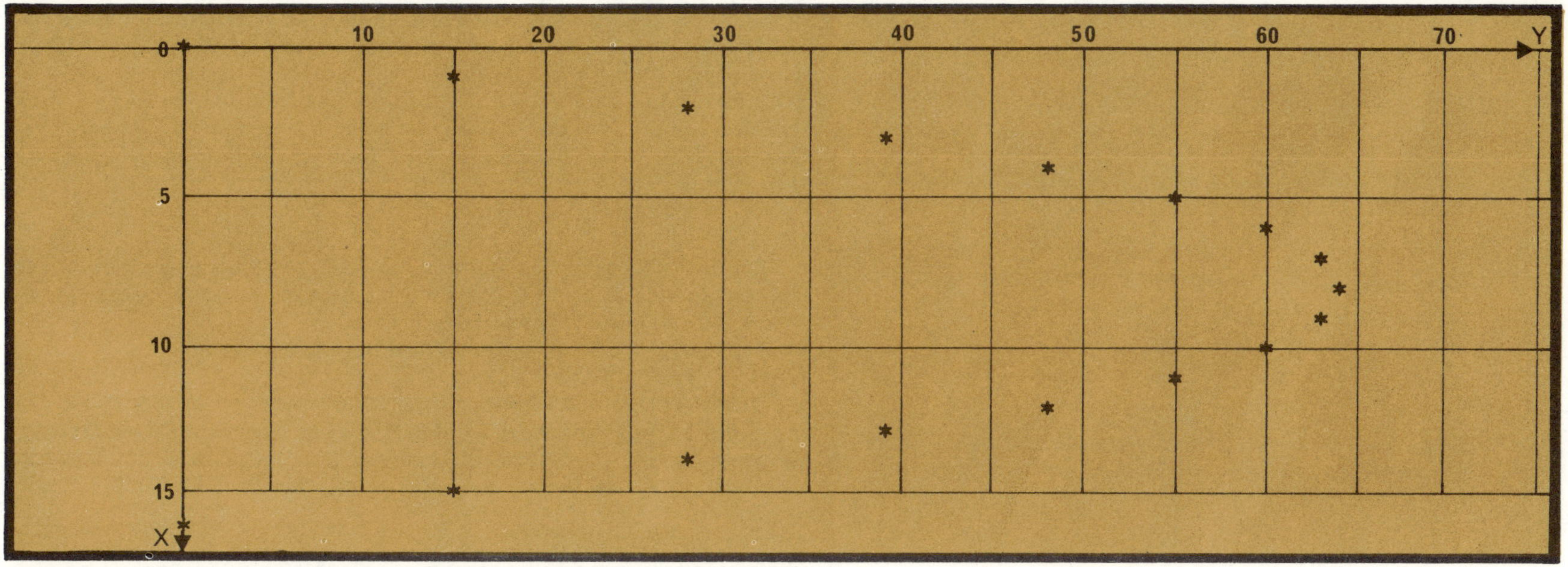

position $5\frac{1}{2}$, but will have to be placed in position 5 or 6. As a result graphs produced by this method sometimes have a slightly uneven look. Before studying Program 15.5, you should look at the graph which it produces. Only the stars are printed by the computer; the axes and scales are added by hand.

The program looks rather complicated, but, once you have understood how it works, you will be able to modify it to plot graphs of many different curves. Let us go through Program 15.5 line by line.

INTEGER BLANK,DOT,SYMBOL

This declaration is necessary as the computer used for this program treats character variables as integers.

DIMENSION SYMBOL(65)

The array **SYMBOL** will store each line of the output until it is printed; each line consists of 64 spaces and one star. (As teleprinters are limited to an output 72 spaces wide, we could use up to **DIMENSION SYMBOL(72)** if necessary; this would be the maximum on our computer, although many computers can output lines with up to 120 characters.)

READ(2,1)BLANK,DOT

This will assign to **DOT** the "value" * and to **BLANK** just a blank space. You will see that the data of the program consist of a blank space followed by *.

DO 2 N = 1,65
SYMBOL(N) = BLANK
2 CONTINUE

This loop assigns to each of the elements of **SYMBOL** the "value" of **BLANK** so that, for example, the instruction **WRITE(3,1)SYMBOL** would produce 65 blank spaces.

DO 3 M = 1,17

This loop will produce the 17 lines that make up the graph. Let us see what happens when we go through the loop for, say, the fifth time, i.e. making **M** equal to 5.

X = M − 1 assigns the value 4.0 to **X.** (**X** was 0 on the first time through the loop.)

Y = X*(16.0 − X) assigns to **Y** the value 48.0. (As the first position on the line corresponds to **Y = 0.0, Y = 48.0** must be in the 49th position.)

I = Y + 1.0 assigns to **I** the value 49.

SYMBOL(I) = DOT assigns to **SYMBOL(49)** the "value" *.

WRITE(3,4)SYMBOL

4 FORMAT(1H ,65A) prints all the 65 elements of **SYMBOL** on one line. Since all the elements of **SYMBOL** are blanks except **SYMBOL(49),** the computer will print a line of blanks with a * in position 49. This corresponds to **Y = 48.0,** since position one, that is **SYMBOL(1),** corresponds to **Y = 0.0.**

SYMBOL(I) = BLANK

This statement changes the "value" of **SYMBOL(49)** from * to a blank space, thus making all the elements of **SYMBOL** blank in preparation for the next cycle of the loop.

The sixth time through the loop (i.e. **M = 6**), the statement **X = M − 1** gives **X** the value 5.0, **Y** the value 55.0 and **SYMBOL(56)** the value *, thus plotting the point (5,55) on the graph.

The axes and scales have been added by hand to avoid making the program too complicated, but in practice a more complicated program would be used to make the computer print out the axes and scales as well.‡

A large computing centre may have a "Library" program for graph plotting. The programmer will input the program together with the function to be plotted, the computer will decide on a suitable scale, and will then output the graph and suitably calibrated axes.

ASSIGNMENT 15.3

1. Re-write Program 15.5 so that it will plot the graph of $y = x\ (12 - x)$ from $x = 0$ to $x = 12$.

2. Describe the output of Program 15.5 if the last two lines were:
   ***DATA**
   − +

‡There is a fuller treatment of graphical output in *A Guide to FORTRAN IV Programming* by D. McCracken; J. Wiley & Sons.

3. If the second **DO** statement in Program 15.5 is changed to **DO 3 M = 1,20,** calculate the values assigned to **X,Y** and **I** in the second **DO** loop when **M** reaches the value 18. Explain what will happen then.

15.4 Plotting Graphs with fractional and negative values for Y

The method used in Program 15.5 will not work for either negative or fractional values of y, since in FORTRAN it is not permissible to have such members of an array as SYMBOL(− 13) or SYMBOL(4.7). It is possible to overcome these difficulties to some extent as shown in Program 15.6, which plots the graph of $y = (x^3 - 15x^2 + 8x + 336)/3$ from $x = -4$ to $x = 14$.

```
C       PROGRAM 15.6
C       GRAPH OF Y=(X**3-15.0*X**2+8.0*X+336.0)/3.0
        INTEGER BLANK, DOT, SYMBOL
        DIMENSION SYMBOL(65)
        READ(2,1)BLANK,DOT
      1 FORMAT(2A1)
        DO 2 N=1,65
        SYMBOL(N)=BLANK
      2 CONTINUE
        DO 3 M=1,19
        X=M-5
        Y=(X**3-15.0*X**2+8.0*X+336.0)/9.0+14.0
        I=Y+0.5
        SYMBOL(I)=DOT
        WRITE(3,4)SYMBOL
      4 FORMAT(1H ,65A1)
        SYMBOL(I)=BLANK
      3 CONTINUE
        END
*DATA
 *
```

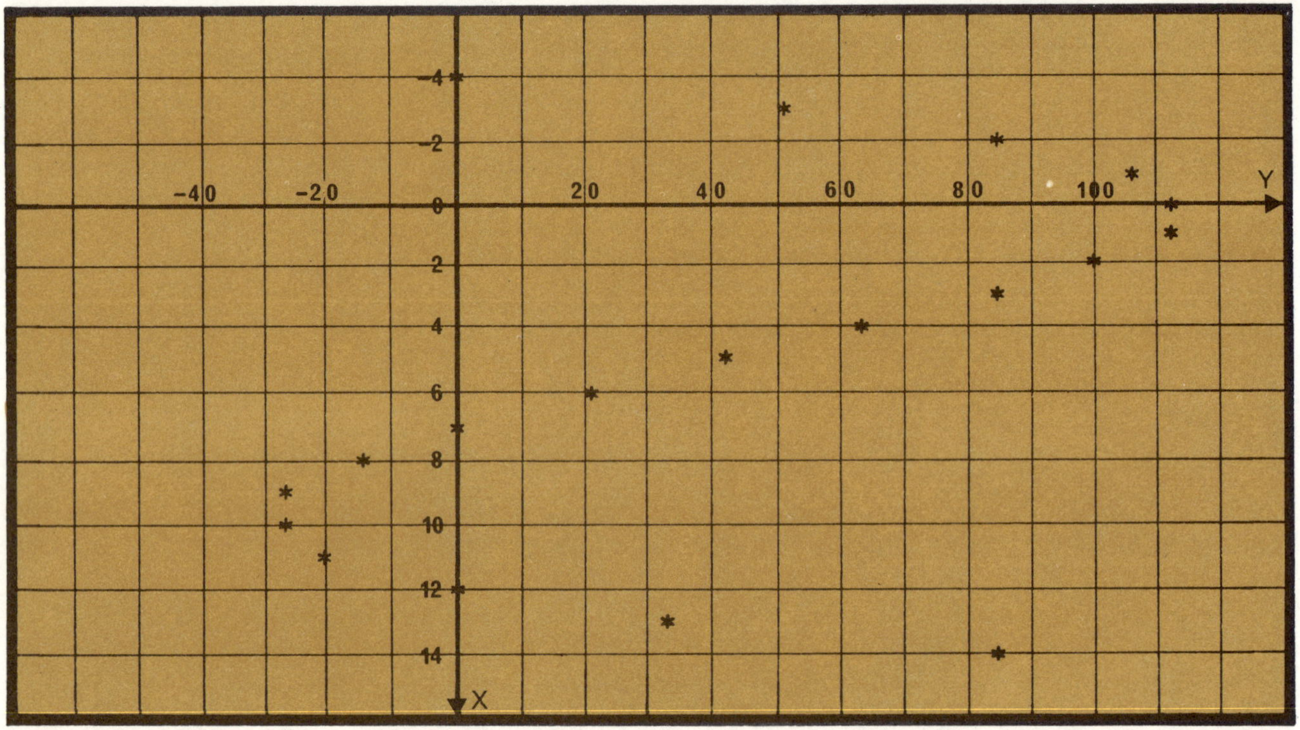

It is first of all necessary to find the range of values of y. There are several ways of doing this. One way is to find the maximum and minimum values using calculus, and another way is to run a short program containing a **DO** loop to work out each value of y.

It will be found that the values of y lie somewhere within the range from -40 to $+140$, which would require about 180 spaces across the page. Since there are only 72 spaces available, however, each space will need to represent three times the value of y. This can be done by using $\frac{1}{3}$ of $(x^3 - 15x^2 + 8x + 336)/3$ in the program as the equation of the curve, making it $y = (x^3 - 15x^2 + 8x + 336)/9$. The effect of the $\frac{1}{3}$ will be to "shrink" the width of the graph to $\frac{1}{3}$ of its original width so that it will fit into the available space. With this reduced scale for y, the range of values will lie somewhere between -13 and 46. We must take steps to ensure that no negative values of y occur when plotting the graph; we do this by adding 14 to each value of y calculated, so that the range of values of y will now be approximately 1 to 60.

Many of the values of y that are calculated will not be whole numbers and will have to be taken to the nearest whole number. This can be done by replacing **I** = **Y** + **1.0** by **I** = **Y** + **0.5.** If, for example, the value of **Y** is 7.3, **I** will be assigned the whole number part of 7.8, that is 7. But if the value of **Y** is, say, 7.8, then **I** will be assigned the whole number part of 8.3, that is 8.

If you look at Program 15.6, you will see that the only difference between it and Program 15.5 is that the second **DO** statement and the three statements after it have been changed. Only these four statements need to be altered to plot almost any graph.

The axes on this graph have been put in by hand. The Y-axis is a horizontal line through the point representing $x = 0$, that is the fifth point down the graph. To find the position of the X-axis, we use the fact that when $x = 0$, $y = 112$. Remembering that each space across the page represents three times the value of y, we have to draw the X-axis 112/3 or 37.3 spaces to the left of this fifth point.

ASSIGNMENT 15.4

1. Show what changes are necessary in Program 15.6 to plot the graph of $y = x^2 - 15$ from $x = -8$ to $x + 8$.
2. Show what changes are necessary in Program 15.6 to plot the graph of $y = x^2 - 15$ from $x = -10$ to $x = +10$.
3. Show what changes are necessary in Program 15.6 to plot the graph of $y = x^2 - 15$ from $x = -10$ to $+10$ by steps of 0.5. (Hint: First alter the **DO** statement.)

ASSIGNMENT 15.5

Write programs to plot the graphs of:

1. $y = x^3 - 4x$ from $x = -5$ to $+5$.
2. $y = 100 - x^2$ from $x = -10$ to $+10$.
3. $y = \sin x + \cos x$ from $-720°$ to $+720°$. Remember to change x to radians (See Unit 12.2).

UNIT
16

The use of Statement Functions in Programs

16.1 In a long program it may be necessary to perform the same kind of calculation many times. For example, it may be necessary to calculate the value of $6x^2 + 45x - 56$ for several values of x. One way of doing this is to use **statement functions.** For the particular case of evaluating $6x^2 + 45x - 56$ the programmer will start his program with **Z(X) = 6.0*X**2 + 45.0*X − 56.0,** and when he wishes to use the statement function, he will **call** it into the program by writing, for example, **A = Z(2.0).** When the computer comes to this statement, it will calculate the value of the expression with **X** equal to 2.0, and then assign this value to **A.** Thus **A** will be assigned the value 58.0.

In another part of the program a variable **P** may have the value 3.0. In this case the statement **F = Z(P)** will instruct the computer to work out the value of the above expression with **X** equal to 3.0; the value of the expression this time is 133.0, and this value will be assigned to **F.** Both of the above calls are illustrated in Program 16.1.

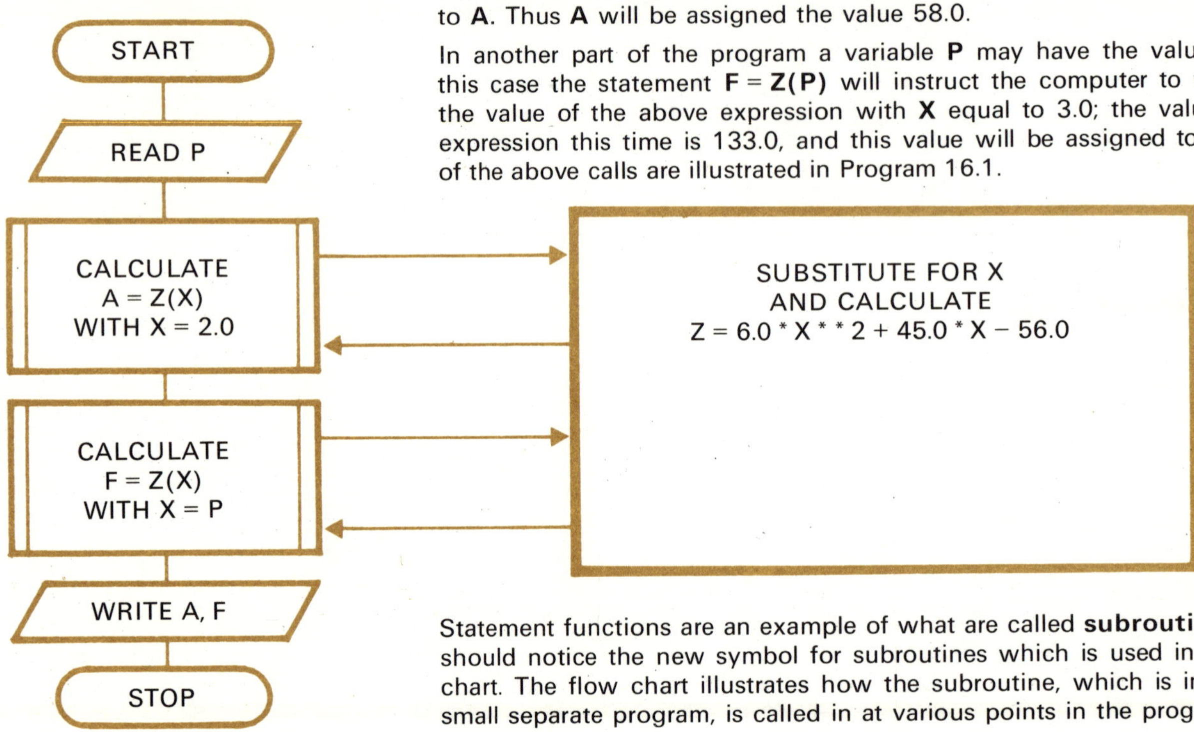

Statement functions are an example of what are called **subroutines;** you should notice the new symbol for subroutines which is used in the flow chart. The flow chart illustrates how the subroutine, which is in effect a small separate program, is called in at various points in the program.

A statement function can be used in a program for many purposes. For example, the statement function **AREA(R) = 3.1415927*R**2** will calculate the area of a circle of radius **R.** If this statement function is placed at the start of a program, the statement **C = AREA(10.0)** will assign to **C** the value 314.15927; or if **H = AREA(D),** and **D** has the value 100.0, **H** will be assigned the value 31415.927.

ASSIGNMENT 16.1

1. What value is assigned to **G** by the following program segment if **Q** has the value 5.0?
   Z(X) = X2 + 3.0**
   G = Z(Q)

2. What value is assigned to **CIRCUM** by this program segment?
   CIRCUM(R) = 3.1416*2.0*R
   R = 5.0
   CIRCUM = CIRCUM(R)

3. If **S** has the value 6.0, what values are assigned to **A** and **X** by this program segment?
   VAL(D) = (D + 3.0)/(D − 3.0)
   A = VAL(9.0)
   X = VAL(S)

```
C       PROGRAM 16.1
C       EXAMPLE OF A STATEMENT FUNCTION.
        Z(X)=6.0*X**2+45.0*X-56.0
        READ(2,1)P
      1 FORMAT(F6.2)
        A=Z(2.0)
        F=Z(P)
        WRITE(3,2)A,F
      2 FORMAT(1H ,2F8.2)
        END
*DATA
  3.0
```

```
     58.00   133.00
```

16.2 Statement Functions of more than one variable

A statement function can contain more than one variable. For example, a program may start with this statement function:
F(A,B,C) = (A2 + B**2 + C**2)/3.0**
The statement
G = F(1.0,2.0,3.0)
will assign to **G** the value (1.0 + 4.0 + 9.0)/3 or 4.6666667.

If **P,Q,R** have the values 0.0,1.0,0.0
H = F(P,Q,R)
will assign to **H** the value 0.333333.

ASSIGNMENT 16.2

1. What value would be assigned to **D** by this program segment?
   AVE(X,Y) = (X + Y)/2.0
   D = AVE(5.0,7.0)

2. If **U** = **10.0** and **V** = **20.0**, what values would be assigned to **A1** and **A2** by the following program segment?
S(X,Y) = SQRT(X*Y)
A1 = S(4.0,9.0)
A2 = 7.0 + 2.0*S(U,V)

It is permissible, as in the last line of this example, to use statement functions in arithmetic assignment statements.

```
C       PROGRAM 16.2
        X(A,B,C,D,E,F)=(E*C-B*F)/(A*E-B*D)
        Y(A,B,C,D,E,F)=(A*F-D*C)/(A*E-B*D)
        READ(2,1)A,B,C,D,E,F
      1 FORMAT(3F10.4)
        U=X(A,B,C,D,E,F)
        V=Y(A,B,C,D,E,F)
        WRITE(3,2)U,V
      2 FORMAT(1H ,2HX=,F10.4/1H ,2HY=,F10.4)
        END
*DATA
      7.0         1.0         9.0
      3.0         2.0         7.0
```

```
  X=      1.0000
  Y=      2.0000
```

*16.3 Solution of a pair of Simultaneous Equations using Statement Functions

It can be shown that the pair of equations
$ax + by = c$
$dx + ey = f$
have solutions
$x = (ec - bf)/(ae - bd) \quad y = (af - dc)/(ae - bd)$.

If we apply these formulae to the equations
$7x + y = 9$
$3x + 2y = 7$
we have the solutions
$x = 1.0 \quad y = 2.0$

Program 16.2 uses a statement function for solving this pair of equations. It should be remembered, however, that this is only a simplified illustration of the use of statement functions. It is in a long program, where there are several sets of equations to solve, that you would make use of a statement function.

When the computer comes to the statement **U = X(A,B,C,D,E,F)**, it takes from its memory the values of **A,B,C,D,E,F** and calculates the value of **(E*C − B*F)/(A*E − B*D)** which is 1.0. It assigns this value to **U**. Similarly when it comes to the statement **V = Y(A,B,C,D,E,F)**, the computer assigns to **V** the value of **(A*F − D*C)/(A*E − B*D)**, which is 2.0.

16.4 Rules for using Statement Functions

When using statement functions, the following rules must be observed:

1. Statement functions, like dimension statements, must always be placed at the start of the program.

2. The name of the function must start with a letter and must not contain more than six characters. (These characters may be letters or numbers or a combination of letters and numbers.) **AVERAGE(A,B) = (A + B)/2.0** is incorrect, but **AVERAG(A,B) = (A + B)/2.0** is correct.

3. Functions having integer results must start with **I,J,K,L,M,N,** and functions not resulting in integers must not start with these letters. **A(I) = J*2 + K*2** is incorrect, but **M(I) = J*2 + K*2** is correct.

4. The names of statement functions must not be the same as those used for FORTRAN supplied functions. For example, since **SQRT(X)** is a supplied function (meaning $\sqrt{X}$), it cannot be used as a statement function; i.e. we may not start a statement function **SQRT(X) =**

*UNIT 17

*Function Subprograms and Subroutine Subprograms

17.1 Function Subprograms

In Unit 16 we studied statement functions which, once defined at the start of a program, could be called upon to perform a given calculation at any point in the program. We are now going to learn about **function subprograms,** which are similar to statement functions, except that they are not limited to single arithmetic assignment statements. For example, at various points in a program we may wish to decrease a number by 10% if it is more than 200, by 5% if its value is from 100 to 200, and to make no change if it is less than 100. A flow chart for this program (Program 17.1) and its associated function subprogram is shown below. The function subprogram is separated from the main program by a dotted line, although this line will not appear on the listing. Flow lines are shown on the listing for the first subprogram call; similar flow lines could be drawn for the other two calls.

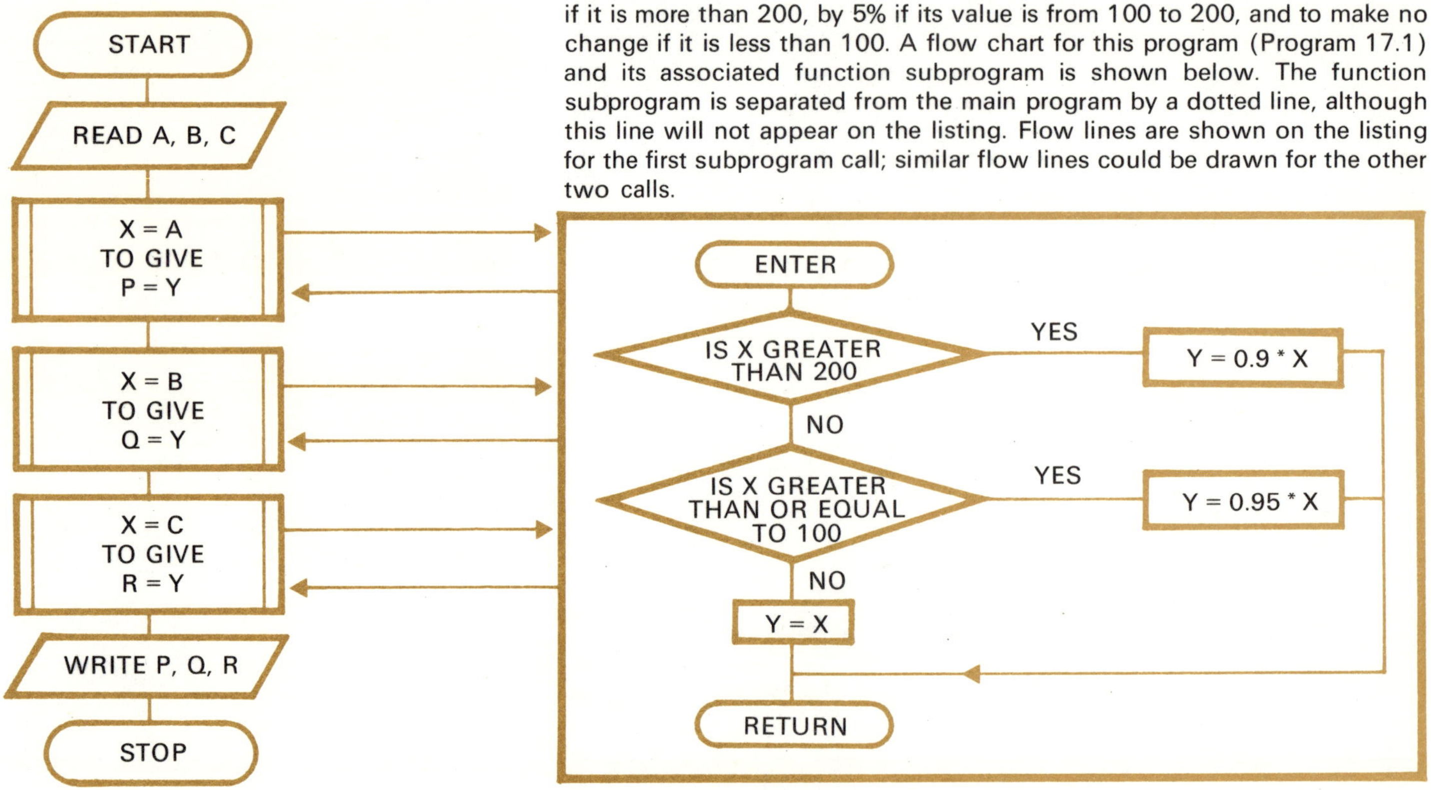

When the computer reads the program, it stores in its memory the function subprogram (which starts at **FUNCTION** and terminates at the first **END**). It then reads the main program. The subprogram is called into use by the statements **P = Y(A)**, **Q = Y(B)** and **R = Y(C)**. At run time the computer first reads the values of **A**, **B** and **C**, and when it comes to the call **P = Y(A)** it takes the entire subprogram from store and uses it with **X** replaced by the value of **A**, in this case 50.0.

Since **A** is less than 100.0, neither of the **GO TO** instructions is followed, and **Y** is assigned the value 50.0. The computer then returns to the main program and assigns to **P** the value of **Y** which has just been calculated.

The computer then comes to the line **Q = Y(B)** and again calls in the subprogram, giving **X** the value 150.0 because 150.0 is the value of **B**. The second **GO TO** is followed and the value 142.5 is assigned to **Y**. The computer then returns to the main program and assigns the value 142.5 to **Q**. In the same way the value 225.0 is assigned to **R**. You will see that the subprogram can **RETURN** to the main program from several points within the subprogram.

The use of subroutines saves program-writing time, punching time and compilation time, although a program containing subroutines usually takes slightly longer to run.

It is possible for a program to contain many function subprograms. One of the advantages of using subprograms is that each of the subprograms may be written and tested separately. In this way the work of writing a very long program can be divided among several programmers.

```
C        PROGRAM 17.1
C        EXAMPLE OF A FUNCTION SUBPROGRAM
         FUNCTION Y(X)
         IF(X.GT.200.0)GO TO 11
         IF(X.GE.100.0)GO TO 12
         Y=X
         RETURN
     11  Y=0.9*X
         RETURN
     12  Y=0.95*X
         RETURN
         END
C        THIS TERMINATES THE SUBPROGRAM
         READ(2,1)A,B,C
      1  FORMAT(3F7.2)
         P=Y(A)
         Q=Y(B)
         R=Y(C)
         WRITE(3,2)P,Q,R
      2  FORMAT(1H ,3F7.2)
         END
*DATA
     50.0   150.0   250.0
```

```
     50.00 142.50 225.00
```

ASSIGNMENT 17.1

1. Write down the output of Program 17.1 if the subprogram is replaced by

```
FUNCTION Y(H)
IF(H.EQ.150.0) Y = H + 50.0
IF(H.NE.150.0) Y = H
RETURN
END
```

2. Write down the output of program 17.1 if the subprogram is replaced by

```
      FUNCTION Y(Z)
      Y = Z
      DO 11 N = 1,3
      X = N
      Y = Y + X
   11 CONTINUE
      RETURN
      END
```

17.2 Example of a Function Subprogram using an Array

```
C       PROGRAM 17.2
        FUNCTION SUM(A,N)
        DIMENSION A(100)
        SUM=0.0
        DO 11 J=1,N
        SUM=SUM+A(J)
     11 CONTINUE
        RETURN
        END
        DIMENSION P(100)
        DO 3 M=1,4
        READ(2,1)P(M)
      1 FORMAT(F5.1)
      3 CONTINUE
        U=SUM(P,4)
        WRITE(3,2)U
      2 FORMAT(1H ,F10.4)
        END
*DATA
  5.0
  3.0
  4.0
  6.0
```

```
    18.0000
```

Function subprograms are often needed in programs containing arrays. Program 17.2 (which finds the sum of the members of an array) contains a subprogram of this type.

In the main program the values of **P** are read, and as there are only four values, only the first four elements of the array are used. The other elements will contain nothing. The computer then comes to **U = SUM(P,4)**, and the subprogram‡ finds the sum of **P(1)** to **P(4)**. Notice that the size of the required **DO** loop must be stated—in this case by putting **N** equal to 4 when the subprogram is called.

The computer goes through the **DO** loop four times, giving **SUM** the value 5.0 the first time, 8.0 the second time, 12.0 the third time, and 18.0 the last time. The computer then returns to the main program and assigns to **U** the value 18.0.

Standard FORTRAN requires the array in the main program to be the same size as the array in the subprogram, but not all versions of FORTRAN impose this restriction. Standard FORTRAN also allows **DIMENSION** statements in subprograms to be of the form **DIMENSION A(N)**, and the value of **N** is part of the call. However, this is beyond the scope of our present studies and we will meet no difficulties provided we remember that a subprogram may be called many times in a long program with a different number of elements used each time; and so it is necessary to make the arrays at least as big as the largest number of elements to be dealt with in the program.

It is possible to have a function subprogram which produces an integer result. In this case we either give an integer name to the subprogram, e.g.
FUNCTION MEAN (I, J, K),
or we declare the function an integer, e.g.
INTEGER FUNCTION AVE(N1, N2).

ASSIGNMENT 17.2

1. Write down the output of Program 17.2 if the subprogram is replaced by

```
    FUNCTION PROD(A,N)
    DIMENSION A(100)
    PROD = 1.0
    DO 11 J = 1,N
    PROD = PROD*A(J)
 11 CONTINUE
    RETURN
    END
```

and if **U = SUM(P,4)** is replaced by **U = PROD(P,4).**

‡ This subprogram is similar to Program 9.3.

2. What value will the statement **M = N(6)** assign to **M** if the statement calls in the following subprogram?

```
    FUNCTION N(I)
    N = O
    DO 11 K = 1,I
    N = N + K
11  CONTINUE
    RETURN
    END
```

3. What value will the statement **M = 10*N(6) + 5** assign to **M** if it calls in the subprogram in the previous question?

4. Subprograms cannot call in themselves. For example, it is incorrect FORTRAN to write M = N(N(6)) using the subprogram in question 2. Can you think of a way of overcoming this difficulty?

17.3 Subroutine Subprograms

In the previous programmes, each time a function subprogram is used, the value of only one variable is calculated. For example, the statement **U = SUM(P,4)** results in a single value being calculated—the value of **U**. Sometimes we need to obtain more than one value as an answer. In order to do this we can use **subroutine subprograms.**

Program 17.3 contains a subroutine subprogram which calculates the values of two variables, the area and the circumference of a circle.

The name of a subroutine cannot have a value assigned to it. We may not, for example, write Y = CIRCLE(3.0,P,Q) and expect to get a value for **Y**. Both the values that we ask in the subroutine and the variables that we calculate must be placed in brackets after the name of the subroutine. In Program 17.3 we will use the value of **R** in the subroutine and calculate the values of **AREA** and **CIRCUM.** The program will be understood better if the flow chart is analysed along with it.

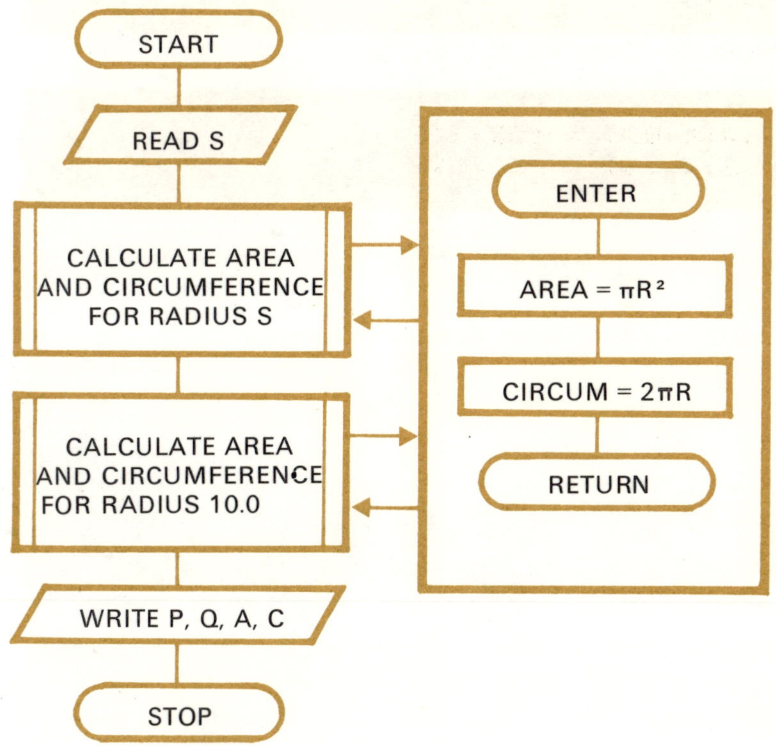

When we wish to call the subroutine into use we write **CALL** followed by the name of the subroutine. In this program, when the subroutine is called for the first time, **R** is assigned the value of **S** and hence the subroutine is carried out with **R** equal to 100.0. The computer calculates the values of **AREA** and **CIRCUM,** proceeds to the main program and assigns the values of **AREA** and **CIRCUM** to **P** and **Q.**

When the subroutine is called for the second time, **R** takes on the value 10.0, the values of **AREA** and **CIRCUM** are again calculated and these new values are assigned to **A** and **C.**

```
C
      PROGRAM 17.3
C     EXAMPLE OF A SUBROUTINE SUBPROGRAM
      SUBROUTINE CIRCLE(R,AREA,CIRCUM)
      AREA=3.1416*R**2
      CIRCUM=2.0*3.1416*R
      RETURN
      END
      READ(2,1)S
    1 FORMAT(F8.2)
      CALL CIRCLE(S,P,Q)
      CALL CIRCLE(10.0,A,C)
      WRITE(3,2)P,Q,A,C
    2 FORMAT(1H ,2F10.3/1H ,2F10.3)
      END
*DATA
 100.0
```

```
  31416.000    628.320
    314.160     62.832
```

You will note that a value can be assigned to **R** either by referring to a variable (in this case **S**), or by stating the value (in this case 10) when the subroutine is called.

The positions of the **arguments** (the letters and numbers) in the subroutine name are of no significance. We may, for example, write
SUBROUTINE CIRCLE(AREA,R,CIRCUM)
provided we also write
CALL CIRCLE (P,S,Q)
CALL CIRCLE (A,10.0,C)

There are two main differences between a function subprogram and a subroutine subprogram:

(1) A subroutine does not produce a value directly like a function. For example, in Program 17.3 if we wished to use the subroutine to calculate the square of the circumference of a circle with radius 7.0 we would first need to give instructions to assign values to the arguments of the subroutine. We could write, say,
CALL CIRCLE(7.0,F,G) followed by
H = G2**

(2) Since a value is not assigned to the name of the subroutine, for example to **CIRCLE,** the first letter does not have to follow the usual rules for **INTEGER** or **REAL.** The only restriction is the usual one that the first symbol is a letter, and that there are not more than six letters and/or numbers in the name.

ASSIGNMENT 17.3

1. Write a subroutine subprogram to calculate the volume and surface area of a sphere. Write the call statement that would be needed to calculate the volume and surface area of a sphere of radius 3.2 and to assign the values of the volume and area to the variables **X** and **Y.**

2. Write down the values that would be assigned to **A** and **I** by **CALL ROOT(2,X,A,I)** used with the following subroutine. **X** has been assigned the value 16.0.

```
SUBROUTINE ROOT(N,Y,P,J)
P = SQRT(Y)
J = N**2
RETURN
END
```

3. Write a subroutine subprogram to assign to **X** the value of the greater of **Y** and **Z.** Write the call statement that would be needed to assign to a variable **H** the greater value of 4.5^3 and 8.2^2.

4. Modify the subroutine in Program 17.3 so that
CALL CIRCLE(10.0,A,C) will produce this output.
RADIUS =   10.0   AREA =   314.15   CIRCUMFERENCE = 62.832

When the **WRITE** instructions are incorporated in the subroutine, a **WRITE** statement is no longer needed in the main program. If you wish to use numbers larger than will fit into the spacing shown, you will need to adjust your **FORMAT** statement. You will need to modify the spacing shown above to allow for larger values being output. (It is allowable to have **WRITE** and **FORMAT** statements in subroutines.)

ASSIGNMENT 17.4

1. Write a subprogram to calculate the volume and surface area of a rectangular box, given the usual three measurements (length, breadth, height).

2. Write a subprogram to calculate the average value of the members of a one dimensional real array. The subprogram should be able to deal with arrays with up to 100 elements.

3. Write a subprogram to find the smallest member of an integer array of one dimension.

4. Write a subprogram to find and print out the largest member of an array of two dimensions.

Solutions

Unlike most problems in mathematics, there are often many possible solutions to even simple problems in computing. For example, in writing a program it makes no difference whether we write 46.00 or 46.0 or even 46. ; and the solution to Assignment 2.4(1) could use **A,B,C,D** in place of **P,Q,R,S**.

The solution given is, where possible, the "best" one, but in correcting your assignments you should bear in mind that there may be several solutions just as correct as the one given.

UNIT 2

Assignment 2.1

1. 45.6
2. 57.0 or 57.
3. 12345.0 or 12345.
4. 34.67
5. 1400.0 or 1400.
6. 45678.57
7. 2867109.0
8. 1.0 or 1.
9. 243.5

You should notice that the 0 after the point is optional.

Assignment 2.2

1. **F10.3**
2. **F10.5**
3. **F9.3**

These are of course the "smallest" answers; the answer to 1 could well be **F12.4** or **F10.4**

4. The two numbers should be spaced **bbb–45.670|bbb357.567**
5. The three numbers should be spaced **b0.56 b0.78 bbb–0.0090**
6. The first line should be **READ(2,8)A,B,C** and there should be no comma in +1,643.2; the 1 should be where the comma is.
7. The first line should be **READ(2,7)P,Q,R** and the **FORMAT** statement number should be 7 and not 8.

Assignment 2.3

1. **b45.78|b–0.78**
2. **bbb–5.9900|b45.7800**
3. **–0.7800|b456.100|bb–5.99000**

Assignment 2.4

1.

```
      READ(2,1)P,Q,R,S
    1 FORMAT(F5.1,F5.1,F5.1,F5.1)
      WRITE(3,2)S,R,Q,P
    2 FORMAT(1H ,F5.1,F5.1,F5.1,F5.1)
      END
*DATA
bb1.2|bb2.3|bb3.4|bb4.5
```

2.
```
      READ(2,10)A,B
   10 FORMAT(F5.2,F5.2)
      WRITE(3,11)A,B
   11 FORMAT(1H ,F5.1,F5.1)
      END
*DATA
b2.57|b3.75
```

3. **M** must not be used for a **REAL** number; another letter, say **Y**, must be used instead.
READ(3,4) should be **READ(2,4)**
WRITE(2,5) should be **WRITE(3,5)**
5 FORMAT(F5.2,F5.2) should be **5 FORMAT(1H ,F5.2,F5.2)**

UNIT 3

Assignment 3.1

1. a. A = 2.0
   b. B = 0.3
   c. C = 200.0
   d. D = 5.0
   e. E = 9.0
   f. F = 400.0
   g. G = − 10.0
   h. H = 218.0

2. a. **U = X**3.0 − Y**3.0**
   b. **V = (X − Y)**3.0**
   c. **W = (A + B)/(A − B)**
   d. **X = 23457.0*C**2.0**
   e. **Y = 0.5*(T + B)*H** or **(T + B)*H/2.0**
   f. **Z = 4.0*3.142*R**3.0/3.0** or **1.333*3.142*R**3.0**

Assignment 3.2

The correct versions are given where possible.

1. **Z = 3.0*X + 4.0*X**
2. **G = 4456.4/Q** Commas not allowed.
3. **H = A*(B + C)**
4. **F = S/2.0**
5. Meaningless FORTRAN expression. See 3.1
6. The expression contains **M**.

Assignment 3.3

1. P = 64.0
2. Q = 81.0
3. A = 5.0
4. S = 3.0
5. X = 40.0
6. X = 100.0
7. Z = 2.0
8. Y = 125.0
9. U = 27.0
10. R = $100^{0.5}$ = square root of 100 = 10.

Assignment 3.4

1.
```
      X = SQRT(10.0)           Missing decimal point.
      Y = SQRT(20.0)           Missing decimal point.
      WRITE(3,1)X,Y            Superfluous comma after Y.
    1 FORMAT(1H ,F10.6,F10.6)  Missing statement number.
      END
*DATA
```

2. No fault will be found when the program is compiled, as each FORTRAN statement is correct in itself, but when the program is run it will produce an incorrect answer. The third line should be **A = (P + Q + R + S)/4.0** and **F10.0** will cut off all the figures after the point in the answer. **F10.4** would be better.

3. No value for **P** is given in the program. We would need either to write 3.142 instead of **P**, or to alter the first two lines to:

```
  READ(2,7)R,P
7 FORMAT(F10.4,F10.4)
```

and put 3.142 after the value of **R** in the data section.
The fourth line should be:
C = 2.0*P*R

Assignment 3.5

1.

```
      READ(2,1)A,B,C,D,E
    1 FORMAT(F10.4,F10.4,F10.4,F10.4,F10.4)
      X = (A + B + C)/(D + E)
      WRITE(3,2)X
    2 FORMAT(1H ,F10.4)
      END
*DATA
```

2. This program uses the fact that the area between the two circles is given by $AREA = \pi P^2 - \pi Q^2$ where P is the radius of the outer circle and Q is the radius of the inner circle.

```
      READ(2,7)P,Q
    7 FORMAT(F10.4,F10.4)
      A = 3.142*P**2.0 - 3.142*Q**2.0
      WRITE(3,8)A
    8 FORMAT(1H ,F10.4)
      END
*DATA
```

3. This program uses the fact that the area is given by $A = 2DW + 2DH + 2WH$ where D;W;H are the length; width and height.

```
      READ(2,10)D,W,H
   10 FORMAT(F8.2,F8.2,F8.2)
      A = 2.0*D*W + 2.0*D*H + 2.0*W*H
      WRITE(3,20)A
   20 FORMAT(1H ,F12.4)
      END
*DATA
```

UNIT 4

Assignment 4.1

1. Starts with **M**.
2. More than six letters or numbers. **VOL5** would be acceptable.
4. Starts with a number. **FIRSTV** would be an acceptable alternative.
6. More than six letters or numbers. **DIAM** would be acceptable.

Assignment 4.2

1. a. FORMAT(1H ,3F5.2)
   b. FORMAT(2F6.3,3F10.4)
   c. FORMAT(1H ,F12.5,2F16.7,F10.4,2F4.1)

2.
```
      READ(2,1)A,B,C,D,E
    1 FORMAT(5F8.4)
      R1 = SQRT(A)
      R2 = SQRT(B)
      R3 = SQRT(C)
      R4 = SQRT(D)
      R5 = SQRT(E)
      WRITE(3,2)R1,R2,R3,R4,R5
    2 FORMAT(1H ,5F8.4)
      END
*DATA
```

UNIT 5

Assignment 5.1

1. 4 FORMAT(2F5.1,I5)
2. 4 FORMAT(1H ,3F5.1,2I5)
3. 6 FORMAT(4I5,F5.1)
4. 9 FORMAT(1H ,2F5.1,3I5,2F5.1)

Assignment 5.2

1. More than six letters or numbers.
2. Does not start with **I, J, K, L, M** or **N**.
4. Starts with a number.

Assignment 5.3

1. M = 9
2. N = 31
3. L = 0
4. M = 64
5. M = 16
6. L = 1
7. L = 0
8. N = − 2

Assignment 5.4

1. I = L + 12
2. J = 1467*M**2
3. S = 4.0*SQRT(4.0)
4. Wrong. The right hand side contains a mixture of real and integer.
5. Wrong. The right hand side contains a mixture of real and integer.

Assignment 5.5

3. You are not allowed to raise an integer to a real power.
4. This is correct FORTRAN, but will assign to **X** the value **3.7**0** or 1. If the statement is designed to calculate the cube root of 3.7, it should be written in the form **X** = **3.7**(1.0/3.0)**
5. You may not raise an integer to a real power.
6. You may not raise an integer to a real power.
8. This is correct FORTRAN, but will assign to **A** the value **0**3** or 0. If it was intended to calculate $\frac{1}{2}$ cubed then it should be **A** = **(1.0/2.0)**3**.

Assignment 5.6

1. I = 2
2. I = 12
3. I = 13
4. J = 13
5. J = 19
6. J = 0

Assignment 5.7

1.
```
      READ(2,1)I
    1 FORMAT(I10)
      X = I
      Y = SQRT(X)
      WRITE(3,2)Y
    2 FORMAT(1H ,F10.4)
      END
*DATA
```

2
```
      READ(2,1)I,J,K,L,M
    1 FORMAT(5I10)
      S = I + J + K + L + M
      AVE = S/5.0
      WRITE(3,2)AVE
    2 FORMAT(1H ,F10.4)
      END
*DATA
```

UNIT 6

Assignment 6.1

1. a. **Y = 5.0**
   b. **M = 10**
   c. **M = 7**
   d. **Y = 5.0**
   e. **Y = 1.5**

2. a. Correct version **IF(X.LE.6.0)**
   b. Mixed **REAL** and **INTEGER** not allowed.
   c. **IF(M.EQ.N)**

Assignment 6.2

1. The computer would continue to output **6 36**; **7 49**; and so on until stopped by the operator.

2. a. Change conditional statement to **IF(N.EQ.20) STOP**
   b. Change **N = 0** to **N = 99**; change **M = N****2** to **M = N****3**; change conditional statement to **IF(N.EQ.200) STOP**.
   c. The change in 2b together with **N = N + 1** changed to **N = N + 2** and **N = 99** to **N = 98.**
   d. Change **N = 0** to **N = 202**; **N = N + 1** to **N = N − 2**; **M = N****2** to **M = N****3**; change conditional statement to **IF(N.EQ.100) STOP.**

3. **20**
   19
   18

Assignment 6.3

1. a. Change second conditional statement to **IF(X.GE.50.0) GO TO 1.**
   b. Change the second conditional statement to **IF(X.LE.70.0) GO TO 1.**
   c. Change the second conditional statement to **IF(X.LT.100.0) GO TO 1** and follow it with **IF(X.GT.200.0) GO TO 1.**

2. a.
```
   73.59
4584.973
    4.4567
```
   b. **73.59**
   c. No output

3. **19**
   2

Assignment 6.4

1.

```
        X = 99.0
      1 X = X + 1.0
        S = SQRT(X)
        Y = X**2
        WRITE(3,2)X,Y,S
      2 FORMAT(1H ,3F10.4)
        IF(X.EQ.120.0) STOP
        GO TO 1
        END
*DATA
```

2.

```
        N = 0
      1 READ(2,2)X
      2 FORMAT(F10.4)
        IF(X.LT.0.0)WRITE(3,3)X
      3 FORMAT(1H ,F10.4)
        N = N + 1
        IF(N.EQ.100) STOP
        GO TO 1
        END
*DATA
```

3.

```
        K = 0
      1 READ(2,2)X,Y
      2 FORMAT(2F10.4)
        DIST = SQRT(X**2 + Y**2)
        IF(DIST.LT.5.0) WRITE(3,3)X,Y
      3 FORMAT(1H ,2F10.4)
        K = K + 1
        IF(K.EQ.10) STOP
        GO TO 1
        END
*DATA
```

UNIT 7

Assignment 7.1

1.
```
bbbb1bbbb1
bbbb2bbbb4
bbbb3bbbb9
```

2.
```
bbbb4bbb16
bbbb7bbb49
bbb10bb100
bbb13bb169
```

3. Same as 2.

4.
```
bbb10bbb16
bbb13bbb19
bbb16bbb22
bbb19bbb25
```

5. Similar to Program 7.1 with the following changes.
```
DO 4 N = 2,5
I = N**3
```

Assignment 7.2

1.

```
        DO 1 I = 1,5
        READ(2,2)X
      2 FORMAT(F10.4)
        Y = SQRT(X)
        WRITE(3,3)X,Y
      3 FORMAT(1H ,2F10.4)
      1 CONTINUE
        END
*DATA
```

2.
```
bb9.5
bb9.2
bb0.0
bb2.0
bb4.0
```

Assignment 7.3

1.
```
      DO 1 M = 51,60
      X = M
      Y = X/10.0
      Z = SQRT(Y)
      WRITE(3,2)Y,Z
    2 FORMAT(1H ,2F10.4)
    1 CONTINUE
      END
*DATA
```

2.
```
      DO 1 N = 1,5
      READ(2,2)J
    2 FORMAT(I10)
      X = J
      Y = 1.1*X
      WRITE(3,3)Y
    3 FORMAT(1H ,F10.1)
    1 CONTINUE
      END
*DATA
```

3.
```
      DO 5 N = 11,19
      X = N
      Y = - X/10.0
      WRITE(3,6)Y
    6 FORMAT(1H ,F5.1)
    5 CONTINUE
      END
*DATA
```

4.
```
bbbb2.0bbb
bbbb5.0bbb
bbbb1.0bbb
bbbb1.3333
bbbb0.5bbb
```

Assignment 7.4

1.
```
      PROD = 1.0
      DO 1 J = 1,5
      READ(2,2)X
    2 FORMAT(F6.2)
      PROD = PROD*X
    1 CONTINUE
      WRITE(3,3)PROD
    3 FORMAT(1H ,F15.5)
      END
*DATA
```

2. Replace line 7 by **SUM = SUM + X**2**
Remove line 9.
Replace **AVE** by **SUM** in line 10.
Replace **F6.2** by say **F12.4** in line 11.

3. Insert the instructions
TOTAL = J
AVE = SUM/TOTAL
WRITE(3,3)AVE
immediately before **CONTINUE** and delete the two lines after **CONTINUE**.

Assignment 7.5

1. Alter the **DO** statement to
DO 1 N = 1,10

2. Insert the following instructions in place of the **WRITE** statement:
X = M
AVE = X/12.0
WRITE(3,3)AVE
and replace **I5** by say **F8.3**

3. **I = 0** to be placed before the **DO** statement.
I = I + M to replace the **WRITE** statement.
WRITE(3,3)I to be placed after **CONTINUE.**

4. Delete everything after **N6** in lines three and five and change **12I3** to **6I3.** The data need not be altered as the computer will ignore the last six columns.

5.
```
      I = 0
      DO 1 J = 1,7
      READ(2,2)K,L
    2 FORMAT(2I2)
      M = K*L
      I = I + M
    1 CONTINUE
      WRITE(3,3)1
    3 FORMAT(1H ,I5)
      END
*DATA
```

Assignment 7.6 1. 3 17 2

2.
```
 441
 784
1225
1764
2401
```

3.
```
1296
2304
3600
```

Assignment 7.7 1.

```
      DO 1 M = 1,20
      READ(2,2)X
    2 FORMAT(F10.4)
      IF(X.LT.0.0) GO TO 3
      S = SQRT(X)
      WRITE(3,4)S
    4 FORMAT(1H ,F10.4)
    3 CONTINUE
    1 CONTINUE
      END
*DATA
```

2.

```
      READ(2,1)N
    1 FORMAT(I5)
      SUM = 0.0
      DO 2 I = 1,N
      READ(2,3)X
      SUM = SUM + X
    2 CONTINUE
      T = N
      AVE = SUM/T
      WRITE(3,4)AVE
    3 FORMAT(F12.4)
    4 FORMAT(1H ,F12.4)
      END
*DATA
```

3. Similar to 2 with the 6th line replaced by **SUM = SUM + X**2.**

4. It is assumed that no numbers larger than 9999 will be read in, and 10000 will be used as the stop number. It is also assumed that the program will not have to deal with more than 1000 numbers.

```
      SUM = 0.0
      DO 1 N = 1,1001
      IF(X.EQ.10000.0) GO TO 3
      READ(2,2)X
      2 FORMAT(F12.4)
      SUM = SUM + X
      T = N
    1 CONTINUE
    3 AVE = SUM/T
      WRITE(3,4)AVE
    4 FORMAT(1H ,F12.4)
      END
*DATA
```

The second program is similar to the above with the fifth line replaced by **SUM = SUM + X**2.**

5. Replace each of the statements containing **SUM** by the following pairs of statements.

```
SUM1 = 0.0
SUM2 = 0.0

IF(X.GT.0.0)SUM1 = SUM1 + X          WRITE(3,4)SUM1
IF(X.LT.0.0)SUM2 = SUM2 - X          WRITE(3,4)SUM2
```

UNIT 8

Assignment 8.1

1. a. FORMAT(2F5.1) b. FORMAT(4F5.1) c. FORMAT(5F5.1)

2. a.
```
1  2  3
4  5  6
```
b.
```
1 2
3 4
5 6
```
c. A single column

d.
```
1 2 3 4
5 6
```
e. 1 2 3 4 5 6

Assignment 8.2

1. a. (2I5/3I5) b. (F5.1,I5/I5,F5.1) c. (3F5.2/3I5) d. (I5/I5/2I5)

2. a.
```
  5.9 24.0
4567–4579
```
b.
```
3456–6785   679
           5709
```

Assignment 8.3

1.
```
      READ(2,1)A,B,C,D,E,F
    1 FORMAT(6F10.4)
      WRITE(3,2)A,B,C,D,E,F
    2 FORMAT(1H ,F10.4)
      END
*DATA
```

2.
```
      READ(2,1)A,B,C,D,E,F
    1 FORMAT(F10.4)
      WRITE(3,2)A,B,C,D,E,F
    2 FORMAT(1H ,6F10.4)
      END
*DATA
```

3.
```
  READ(2,1)A,B,C,D,E,F,G,H,P
1 FORMAT(3F10.4)
```

UNIT 9

Assignment 9.1

1. a. 1.0 2.0 3.0

b.
```
2  5  7
3  8  9
```

2. Change **FORMAT** to **(1H ,I5)**

3. a.
```
 100
 400
 900
1600
```
b. 455.67 –4.89 46.4 0.87 –56.8 4.11

c. 3 6 9 12 15

Assignment 9.2

1. a. Change **6F8.2** to **F8.2**
   b. Change **6F8.2** to **F8.2** and **6** to **500** in the **DIMENSION** and **DO** statements.
   c. Change **SUM = 0.0** to **SUM = 1.0**, and **SUM = SUM + X(N)** to **SUM = SUM*X(N)**
   d. Change **SUM = SUM + X(N)** to **SUM = SUM + X(N)**2**
   e. Change **6F8.2** to **8F8.2** and **6** to **400** in the **DIMENSION** and **DO** statements

Assignment 9.3

1.

```
      DIMENSION X(100),Y(100)
      READ(2,1)X
    1 FORMAT(F10.4)
      DO 2 N = 1,100
      Y(N) = 2.4*X(N)
    2 CONTINUE
      WRITE(3,3)Y
    3 FORMAT(1H ,F10.4)
      END
*DATA       (To be arranged in column form)
```

2.

```
      DIMENSION P(50),Q(50),R(50),T(50)
      READ(2,1)P,Q,R
    1 FORMAT(F10.4)
      DO 2 I = 1,50
      T(I) = P(I) + Q(I) + R(I)
    2 CONTINUE
      WRITE(3,3)T
    3 FORMAT(1H ,F10.4)
      END
*DATA       (To be arranged in column form, firstly P, then Q, then R)
```

3.

```
      DIMENSION M(20)
      READ(2,1)M
    1 FORMAT(I10)
      N = 0
      DO 2 K = 1,20
      N = N + M(K)
    2 CONTINUE
      TOTAL = N
      AVE = TOTAL/20.0
      WRITE(3,3)AVE
    3 FORMAT(1H ,F10.4)
      END
*DATA       (To be arranged in column form)
```

4.

```
      DIMENSION I(200), J(200)
      READ(2,1)I
    1 FORMAT(I10)
      DO 2 N = 1,200
      K = 201 - N
      J(N) = I(K)
    2 CONTINUE
      WRITE(3,3)J
    3 FORMAT(1H ,I10)
      END
*DATA
```

When the **DO** loop is executed for say the 4th time, then **K** is assigned the value 197 and the following statement becomes **J(4) = I(197).** In other words the 4th member of **J** is the 197th member of **I,** and so on.

5. The formula used is $\sigma = \sqrt{\frac{\Sigma x^2}{n} - \left(\frac{\Sigma x}{n}\right)^2}$

where Σx means the sum of all the x's, and Σx^2 means the sum of the squares of the x's.

```
      DIMENSION X(100)
      READ(2,1)X
    1 FORMAT(F10.4)
      SUM1 = 0.0
      SUM2 = 0.0
      DO 2 I = 1,100
      SUM1 = SUM1 + X(I)
      SUM2 = SUM2 + X(I)**2
    2 CONTINUE
      SD = SQRT((SUM2/100.0) - (SUM1/100.0)**2)
      WRITE(3,3)SD
    3 FORMAT(1H ,F10.4)
      END
*DATA
```

UNIT 10

Assignment 10.1 1. FORMAT(1H ,I5,I9)

2.
```
      WRITE(3,1)
    1 FORMAT(1H ,29HCUBES AND SQUARES OF INTEGERS//1H ,19HINTEGER SQUARE CUBE)
```

3.
```
ABCDE
FGHIJ

KLMNO


PQRST
```

4.
```
      WRITE(3,2)
    2 FORMAT(1H ,16HTABLE OF SQUARES/1H ,9HAND CUBES)
```

```
TABLE OF SQUARES
AND CUBES
```

Assignment 10.2

1. FORMAT(1H ,3HONE,7X,3HTWO,7X,5HTHREE,5X,4HFOUR/1H ,4HFIVE,6X,3HSIX
   1,7X,5HSEVEN,5X,5HEIGHT/1H ,4HNINE,6X,3HTEN)

2. FORMAT(1H ,5HZZZZZ/1H ,2H Z/1H ,3H Z/1H 4H   Z)

3. bbbbbSQUARE ROOTS OF NUMBERS FROM 1 TO 10

   bbbbbbbbbb NUMBER ROOT

Assignment 10.3

```
   WRITE(3,1)
 1 FORMAT(1H ,69HSQUARES,SQUARE ROOTS,CUBES AND CUBE ROOTS OF INTEGER
  1S FROM 100 TO 150//1H ,51HINTEGER   SQUARE   SQUARE ROOT    CUBE
  2  CUBE ROOT)
   DO 3 N = 100,150
   X = N
   M = N**2
   I = N**3
   S = SQRT(X)
   C = X**(1.0/3.0)
   WRITE(3,2)N,M,S,I,C
 3 CONTINUE
 2 FORMAT(1H ,I7,I9,F14.8,I9,F12.8)
   END
*DATA
```

This will give the following output:

SQUARES,SQUARE ROOTS,CUBES AND CUBE ROOTS OF INTEGERS FROM 100 TO 150

INTEGER	SQUARE	SQUARE ROOT	CUBE	CUBE ROOT
100	10000	10.00000000	1000000	4.64158883

. . . .

2.

```
   WRITE(3,1)
 1 FORMAT(1H ,40HAREAS AND CIRCUMFERENCES OF CIRCLES WITH/1H ,46HRADI
  1I FROM 0.1 CM TO 1.0 CM IN STEPS OF 0.1 CM//1H ,31HRADIUS     AREA
  2     CIRCUMFERENCE)
   DO 2 N = 1,10
   X = N
   R = X/10.0
   A = 3.14159*R**2
   C = 2.0*3.14159*R
   WRITE(3,3)R,A,C
 3 FORMAT(1H ,F6.1,F8.5,F17.5)
 2 CONTINUE
   END

*DATA
```

This will give the following output:—

```
AREAS AND CIRCUMFERENCES OF CIRCLES WITH
RADII FROM 0.1 CM TO 1.0 CM IN STEPS OF 0.1 CM
RADIUS      AREA       CIRCUMFERENCE
    0.1    0.03142           0.62832
. . . . . . . . . . . . . . . . .
```

UNIT 11

Assignment 11.1

1.
```
      WRITE(3,5)PROFIT,COST,SALE
    5 FORMAT(1H ,7HPROFIT = ,F6.2,7H   COST = ,F6.2,7H   SALE = ,
     1F6.2)
```

2.
```
      WRITE(3,5)PROFIT,COST,SALE
    5 FORMAT(1H ,7HPROFIT = ,F6.2/1H ,7HCOST =   ,F6.2/1H ,7HSALE =   ,F6.2)
```

3.
```
      WRITE(3,5)PROFIT,COST,SALE
    5 FORMAT(1H ,25HTHE PROFITS AND COSTS ARE,F6.2,4H AND,
     1F6.2,8H DOLLARS/1H ,25X,10HSALE PRICE,F6.2,8H DOLLARS)
```

Assignment 11.2

1.
```
      WRITE(3,3)LP,L,P
    3 FORMAT(1H ,22HBATH  BRIS  GLOU  LEED/1H ,4I6,10H   PREVIOUS/1H ,4I6
     1,6H   LAST/1H ,4F6.2,10H   INCREASE)
```

2.
```
      DIMENSION I(10), R(10)
      READ(2,1)I
    1 FORMAT(10I6)
      DO 2 N = 1,10
      X = I(N)
      R(N) = SQRT(X)
    2 CONTINUE
      WRITE(3,3)I,R
    3 FORMAT(1H ,7HINTEGER,10I6/1H ,7HSQRT   ,10F6.2)
      END
*DATA
```

(The ten numbers are arranged in a row, six spaces to each number.)

3.
```
      WRITE(3,1)
    1 FORMAT(1H ,24HSQUARE ROOTS OF INTEGERS//1H ,21HINTEGER   SQUARE RO
     1OT)
      DO 2 J = 1,10
      READ(2,3)N
    3 FORMAT(I5)
      X = N
      Y = SQRT(X)
      WRITE(3,4)N,Y
    4 FORMAT(1H ,I5,F13.2)
    2 CONTINUE
      END
*DATA
```

Assignment 12.1

1.
```
    READ(2,1)AC,A
  1 FORMAT(2F10.4)
    BC = AC*SIN(0.017453*A)
```
and then the same as before with the data inserted.

2. Change **SIN** to **COS**

Assignment 12.2

1. **Z = 3.0** 2. **M = 21** 3. **Y = 10.0**

4. Incorrect statement. It should be **L = IABS(− 5)** giving **L** the value 5.

Assignment 12.3

1. Second approximation = 4.5, third and subsequent approximations = 4.47.

2. Replace **STOP** by **GO TO 4**, delete the **WRITE** statement, and insert **4 WRITE(3,3)A** after **GO TO 2**.

3. For real values you could use **Y = SQRT(X**2)**. For integer values you could use
```
X = N**2
I = SQRT(X)
```
Alternatively **IF(X.LT.0.0)X = —X** could be used for real numbers, and **IF(N.LT.0)N = − N** could be used for integers.

Assignment 12.4

1.
```
      DO 1 N = 1,10
    3 READ(2,2)X
    2 FORMAT(F10.4)
      IF(X.GE.0.0)GO TO 3
      X = ABS(X)
      WRITE(3,4)X
    4 FORMAT(1H ,F10.4)
    1 CONTINUE
      END
*DATA
```

2.
```
      DO 1 N = 60,69
      A = N
      BC = 3.64*SIN(0.017453*A)
      WRITE(3,2)BC
    2 FORMAT(1H ,F10.4)
    1 CONTINUE
      END
*DATA
```

3.
```
      READ(2,1)X,A
    1 FORMAT(F10.4)
      DO 2 N = 1,10
      Y = A
      A = (A + X/A)/2.0
      WRITE(3,3)A
    3 FORMAT(1H ,F10.6)
      IF(ABS(Y − A).LT.0.0000001)STOP
    2 CONTINUE
      END
*DATA
```

Assignment 13.1

1. Change the **4** in the **DO** and **DIMENSION** statements to **400.**
2. Alter the statement starting **Y(N)** to **Y(N) = SQRT(X(N)).**

Assignment 13.2

1. Change **30** and **32** in the **DO** statements to **10** and **15.**
2. Same changes as above plus **I = M*N** replaced by
   X = M
   Y = N
   X = X/10.0
   Y = Y/10.0
   Z = X*Y
   Replace **M,N,I** in **WRITE** statement by **X,Y,Z** and replace **I5; I4; I5** in **FORMAT** statement by, say, **F5.1 ; F5.1 ; F6.2.**
3.

```
      DO 1 N = 61,64
      DO 2 M = 61,63
      X = N
      X = X/10.0
      Y = M
      Y = Y/10.0
      Z = X*Y
      WRITE(3,3)Y,X,Z
    3 FORMAT(1H  ,F6.2,6H  TIMES,F6.2,7H  EQUALS,F6.2)
    2 CONTINUE
    1 CONTINUE
      END
*DATA
```

Assignment 13.3

1. Change **30,32** to **10,15** in the first **DO** statement. **3** to **6** in the second **DO** statement, and in the **DIMENSION** statement. Alter the statement starting **K(M)** to **K(M) = (M + 9)*N** and change **3I5** in the **FORMAT** statement to **6I5.**
2. Change **3I5** to **I5** in the **FORMAT** statement.

Assignment 13.4

1. Change the **5** to **10** in the **DIMENSION,** and **DO** statements. Change the first **FORMAT** statement to **FORMAT(1H ,5X,3H0.1,4X,3H0.2,4X,3H0.3,4X,** etc.
   Insert after **Y = M**
   X = X/10.0
   Y = Y/10.0
   Change the two statements after **2 CONTINUE** to

```
  WRITE(3,3)X,H
3 FORMAT(1H  ,F4.1,10F7.3)
```

2\. 1
1
2
1
2
3

3\. Insert after the dimension statement

```
      WRITE(3,4)
    4 FORMAT(1H ,8X,12H30     31     32)
```

and insert in place of the **FORMAT** and **WRITE** statements

```
      WRITE(3,3)N,K
    3 FORMAT(1H ,4I5)
```

Assignment 13.5 1.

```
      DIMENSION W(5)
      DO 1 I=10,20
      X=I
      D=X/10.0
      WRITE(3,2)D
    2 FORMAT(1H1,23HMASS OF CONE OF DENSITY,F4.1,11H GMS PER CC//1H ,30X
     1,10HHEIGHT   CMS//1H  ,10HRADIUS  CMS,5X,1H2,9X,1H4,9X,1H6,9X,1H8,8X,2
     2H10)
      DO 3 J=1,10
      R=J
      DO 4 K=1,5
      H=2*K
      W(K)=3.14159*R**2*H*D/3.0
    4 CONTINUE
      WRITE(3,5)J,W
    5 FORMAT(1H  ,I6,4X,5F10.4)
    3 CONTINUE
    1 CONTINUE
      END
*DATA
```

The first line of the output of the sixth page is given below.

```
MASS OF CONE OF DENSITY 1.5 GMS PER CC

                                 HEIGHT CMS

RADIUS CMS     2          4          6          8         10
     1      3.1416     6.2832     9.4248    12.5664    15.7080
. . . . . . . . . . . . . . . . . . . . . . . . . . . . . . .
```

Assignment 14.1

1.

```
      DIMENSION I(3,3)
      READ(2,1) I
    1 FORMAT(3I5)
      WRITE(3,2) I(1,1),I(2,2),I(3,3)
    2 FORMAT(1H ,3I5)
      END
*DATA
```

2.

```
      DIMENSION A(4,3)
      READ(2,1) A
    1 FORMAT(4F5.1)
      WRITE(3,2)A(1,2),A(2,2),A(3,2),A(4,2)
      WRITE(3,3)A(4,1),A(4,2),A(4,3)
    2 FORMAT(1H ,4F5.1)
    3 FORMAT(1H ,F5.1)
      END
*DATA
```

Assignment 14.2

1. Change to **J(N) = M(N,2)**

2. Insert immediately before the existing **DO** statement of Program 14.3.

```
      DO 4 N = 1,5
      J(N) = M(N,2)
    4 CONTINUE
      WRITE(3,3)J
```

3. Exchange the position of the **DO** loops in the solution to Question 2.

4. Replace the **DO** loop by

```
      DO 2 N = 1,3
      WRITE(3,3)M(2,N),M(4,N)
    3 FORMAT(1H ,2I5)
    2 CONTINUE
```

and delete the second **FORMAT** statement.

Assignment 14.3

1. Change **N = N + L(2,I)** to **N = N + L(4,I)**

2. Change the **3** to **4** in the **DO** statement, and change **N = N + L(2,I)** to **N = N + L(I,3)**

3. Change to **DIMENSION L(10,10)**
Change the **3** to **10** in the **DO** statement.
Change **N = N + L(2,I)** to **N = N + L(I,7)**

4.

```
      DIMENSION I(10,20)
      READ(2,2) I
    2 FORMAT(10I5)
      DO 1 N = 1,20
      DO 3 J = 1,10
      I(J,N) = I(J,N)**2
    3 CONTINUE
    1 CONTINUE
      WRITE(3,4) I
    4 FORMAT(1H ,10I5)
      END
*DATA
```

Assignment 14.4

1.
```
      READ(2,1)J
    1 FORMAT(14I5)
```

2. Insert after 1 CONTINUE
```
      VALUE = 0.0
      DO 5 N = 1,3
      VALUE = VALUE + RVALUE(N)
    5 CONTINUE
      WRITE(3,6) VALUE
    6 FORMAT(1H  ,F10.2)
```

Assignment 14.5

```
      REAL I,J,K
      INTEGER X,Y,Z
```

UNIT 15

Assignment 15.1

1. FREDbbOXObbbTEDbbbBRANDY
(The b's indicate the number of blanks.)

2.
```
. . .
XXX
*  *
```

Assignment 15.2

1.
```
      DIMENSION N(10)
      READ(2,1)N
    1 FORMAT(10A6)
      WRITE(3,2)N
    2 FORMAT(1H  ,A6)
      END
*DATA
```

2.
```
      DIMENSION N(10),M(10)
      READ(2,1)N
    1 FORMAT(10A1)
      DO 2 I = 1,10
      M(I) = N(11 - I)
    2 CONTINUE
      WRITE(3,3)M
    3 FORMAT(1H  ,10A1)
      END
*DATA
```

3.
```
      DIMENSION N(10,10), M(10,10)
      READ(2,1)N
    1 FORMAT(10A1)
      DO 2 I = 1,10
      DO 3 J = 1,10
      M(I,J) = N(J,I)
    3 CONTINUE
    2 CONTINUE
      WRITE(3,4)M
    4 FORMAT(1H  ,10A1)
      END
*DATA
```

Assignment 15.3

1. Change the second **DO** statement to **DO 3 M = 1,13** and replace the function by **Y = X*(12.0 – X)**.
2. The graph would be plotted as + signs on a background of – signs.
3. When **M = 18**, we would have **X = 17.0** and **Y = – 17.0**. This would give **I** the value – 16, and since **SYMBOL(– 16)** has no meaning in FORTRAN, the computer would stop executing the program, although it would have printed the graph up to **X = 16.0**.

Assignment 15.4

1. Change the three statements after **2 CONTINUE** to
   DO 3 N = 1,17
   X = N – 9
   Y = X2 + 1.0**
   16 has been added to $y = x^2 - 15$ so that y is never negative.
2. Change the three statements after **2 CONTINUE** to
   DO 3 N = 1,21
   X = N – 11
   Y = (X2 – 15.0)/2.0 + 8.0**
   $x^2 - 15$ has been divided by 2 to keep the range of the values of y to under 72, and 8.0 has been added to keep the value of y positive.
3. Change the three statements after **2 CONTINUE** to
   DO 3 N = 10,210,5
   X = N – 110
   X = X/10.0
   Y = (X2 – 15.0)/2.0 + 8.0**

Assignment 15.5

Assuming that the output is on a teleprinter with 72 print positions we could first change the 65 to 72 in the **DIMENSION** and first **DO** statement in Program 15.6

We now need to change the second **DO** statement and the two following statements as follows.

1. **DO 3 M = 1,11**   2. **DO 3 M = 1,21**
3. **DO 3 M = 1,73**   (We are calculating in steps of 20°.)

1. **X = M – 6**   2. **X = M – 11**   3. **X = 20*(M–37)**

1. **Y = (X**3 – 4.0*X)/4.0 + 27.25**
   This will change the original range of y (– 105 to + 105) to 1 to 53.4.
2. **Y = (100.0 – X**2)/2.0 + 1.0**
   This will change the original range of y (0 to 100) to 1 to 51.
3. **Y = 20.0*(SIN(0.017453*X) + COS(0.017453*X)) + 29.0**
   This will change the original range of y (– 1.414 to + 1.414) to 0.72 to 57.28.

UNIT 16

Assignment 16.1 1. G = 28.0 2. CIRCUM = 31.416 3. A = 2.0, X = 3.0

Assignment 16.2 1. D = 6.0 2. A1 = 6.0, A2 = 7.0 + 2.0*SQRT(200.0) = 35.247

UNIT 17

Assignment 17.1

1. 50.00 200.00 250.00
2. 56.00 156.00 256.00

Assignment 17.2

1. 360.0000
2. 21
3. 215
4. The subprogram could be stated twice at the start of the program. We could in this case follow the first subprogram by a second starting **FUNCTION L(I)**. Then, instead of writing **M = N(N(6))** which is not valid FORTRAN, we could write **M = L(N(6))**. Or, we could write **I = N(6)** followed by **M = N(I)**.

Assignment 17.3

1.
```
SUBROUTINE SPHERE(R,V,A)
A = 4.0*3.14159*R**2
V = 4.0*3.14159*R**3/3.0
RETURN
END
```
This is called in with **CALL SPHERE(3.2,X,Y)**

2. **A = 4.0, I = 4**

3.
```
SUBROUTINE MAX(Y,Z,X)
X = Y
IF(Z.GT.Y)X = Z
RETURN
END
```
This is called in with **CALL MAX(4.5**3,8.2**2,H)**

4.
```
   SUBROUTINE CIRCLE(R,AREA,CIRCUM)
   AREA = 3.14159*R**2
   CIRCUM = 2.0*3.14159*R
   WRITE(3,1)R,AREA,CIRCUM
 1 FORMAT(1H ,7HRADIUS = ,F10.3,6H  AREA = ,F10.3,15H CIRCUMFERENCE = ,F10.3)
   RETURN
   END
```

Assignment 17.4

1.
```
SUBROUTINE BOX(VOL,AREA,D,W,H)
VOL = D*W*H
AREA = 2.0*(D*W + W*H + H*D)
RETURN
END
```
this is called in with say
CALL(P,Q,X,Y,Z)
where **X,Y,Z** are the measurements of the box, and **P** will be assigned the value of the volume of the box, and **Q** the value of the area.

2. Similar to Program 17.2 with **SUM** replaced by say, **AVE** in lines 2 and 13, and with
T = N
AVE = SUM/T inserted after **CONTINUE.**

3.
```
     FUNCTION MIN(I,N)
     DIMENSION I(2000)
     MIN = I(1)
     DO 1 I = 1,N
     IF(I(N).LT.MIN)  MIN = I(N)
   1 CONTINUE
     RETURN
     END
```
This is called in with say
J = MIN(K,30)
where **K** is an **INTEGER** array (**DIMENSION K(2000)** will be required at the start of the main program). **J** will be assigned the value of the least member of the array **K.**

4.
```
     FUNCTION MAX(I,J,N)
     DIMENSION I(50,50)
     MAX = I(1,1)
     DO 1 K = 1,J
     DO 2 M = 1,N
     IF(I(J,N).GT.MAX) MAX = I(J,N)
   2 CONTINUE
   1 CONTINUE
     WRITE(3,3) MAX
   3 FORMAT(1H  ,I10)
     RETURN
     END
```
This is called in with say,
I1 = MAX(MEAN,5,7)
where **MEAN** is a 5 by 7 array and is declared with **DIMENSION MEAN (50,50)** at the start of the main program. **I1** will be assigned the value of the largest member of the array, and the subprogram will also output this value.